CHINESE OPERA

Siu Wang-Ngai

with

Peter Lovrick

Chinese Opera

Images and Stories

UBC Press / Vancouver

University of Washington Press / Seattle

ISBN 0-7748-0592-7

Canadian Cataloguing in Publication Data

Siu, Wang-Ngai, 1938-
    Chinese opera

    Includes some text in Chinese.
    Includes bibliographical references and index.
    ISBN 0-7748-0592-7

    1. Operas, Chinese – Stories, plots, etc. 2. Operas,
Chinese – History and criticism. 3. Operas, Chinese
– Pictorial works. I. Lovrick, Peter, 1953- II. Title.
ML1751.C4S58 1997   782.1'0951   C96-910495-2

UBC Press gratefully acknowledges the ongoing sup-
port to its publishing program from the Canada
Council, the Province of British Columbia Cultural
Services Branch, and the Department of
Communications of the Government of Canada.

Title page: The White Eel Fairy in *Delights of the
Mortal World*, Sichuan opera, photograph by Siu
Wang-Ngai

UBC Press
University of British Columbia
6344 Memorial Road
Vancouver, BC V6T 1Z2
(604) 822-3259
Fax: 1-800-668-0821
E-mail: orders@ubcpress.ubc.ca
http://www.ubcpress.ubc.ca

Published simultaneously in the United States of
America by the University of Washington Press,
P.O. Box 50096, Seattle, WA 98145-5096

ISBN 0-295-97610-1

Library of Congress Cataloging-in Publication Data

Siu, Wang-Ngai, 1938-
    Chinese opera : images and stories / Siu Wang-
Ngai, with Peter Lovrick.
        p.   cm.
    Includes bibliographical references and index.
    ISBN 0-295-97610-1 (alk. paper)
    1. Operas, Chinese – History and criticism. I.
Lovrick, Peter, 1953-   . II. Title.
ML1751.C4S58 1997   96-39596
782.1'0951 – dc21   CIP
                                              MN

Distributed in Hong Kong, Macau, the PRC,
Singapore, and Taiwan by Asia Publishers Services
Limited, 16/F Wing Fat Commercial Building,
218 Aberdeen Main Road, Aberdeen, Hong Kong
(fax: 2554-2912).

Contents

Preface

Peter Lovrick

TWO YEARS AGO, Kate Stevens gave me a call from her home in Victoria, British Columbia. It would plunge me into a fascinating, sometimes irritating, but ultimately rewarding project. Professor Stevens taught in the Department of East Asian Studies at the University of Toronto until her retirement in the late 1980s. She taught Chinese performing arts as literature for over twenty years and has made an extensive study of Peking drum singing, a storytelling genre which she performs. I had been and, in the Chinese way of looking at things, still was her student. After she left the university, I continued as a teacher of Performing Arts in China in her place, a post for which she recommended me. Now, she had something else on her mind for me. Would I be interested in writing a book on Chinese opera? A book? Surely, there were quite a number of these already. But what Kate Stevens had in mind was something quite different. That's when she told me about Siu Wang-Ngai and his collection of photographs.

Siu Wang-Ngai is one of the most prominent photographers in Hong Kong. A lawyer by profession, he has won international recognition for his photographs. The Royal Photographic Society of Great Britain awarded him a fellowship for his theatrical photography in 1985, and honoured him with a second fellowship in 1989 for his pictorial photography. Mr. Siu's photographs are frequently exhibited and published. He was chair of the Federation of Hong Kong-Macao Photographic Associations and often serves as a judge in Hong Kong photography exhibitions. Kate Stevens explained that one of Siu's ongoing special projects was photographing Chinese regional opera. There are over 300 different regional opera styles in China. In recent years, outstanding troupes with China's foremost performers have visited Hong Kong. Siu began photographing their performances in 1981 and has so far taken over 30,000 photographs of more than 200 operas in twenty-two regional opera styles. These photographs were what would make this book special. Siu was prepared to select a number of shots from his collection personally, but they needed text around them to explain the stories and give background. I was intrigued. In addition to my teaching work, I performed the painted-face role in the Chinese Opera Group of Toronto. I knew what it felt like, if only as an amateur, to wear the bold make-up, carry the heavy costume, and tell a story using conventions from a highly polished theatrical tradition. Maybe I could bring that experience to the photographs.

A month later I flew out to Vancouver to meet Siu. He turned out to be a quiet, unassuming man. As I got to know him better, I discovered that he was both gracious and considerate. He was accompanied by Kwan Lihuen, a charming gentleman who delighted me with his conversation on *taijiquan* (or *tai chi chuan*, a form of slow exercise), Chinese philosophy, and teaching English to Chinese speakers. Kwan, it seemed, had been instrumental in promoting the idea that Siu's photos should be published.

I first saw those photographs spread out over tables in the offices of UBC Press. Kate Stevens, Siu Wang-Ngai, and I looked at them to see what kind of shape they might take. They were remarkable. Aside from major opera styles, Siu had captured regional operas that are rarely seen outside of China and are in decline even in China itself. His method was to shoot the plays in performance. He looked for particularly dramatic images in which gesture and facial expression conveyed both the theatrical moment and the flavour of the regional opera style. He used no flash or tripod. The result was a series of photographs that, in contrast to posed studio shots, conveyed vital and living operas in performance. The operas covered a broad range from historical dramas to ghost stories.

The first question to settle was audience. For whom was this book intended? From the start, we decided that it was not to be a scholarly work meant for specialists in Chinese studies. For a broader appeal, we decided not to assume a background in Chinese theatre. This meant, then, providing an historical overview to furnish the context of the operas. An anecdotal history of Chinese opera is therefore provided in Chapter 1. It also meant introducing the regional differences and stage conventions of Chinese theatre. The conventions are taken for granted by a seasoned opera audience but are quite foreign to most Western audiences, raised in realism. Chapters 2 and 3 cover regional variations and general operatic conventions. But what about the main matter, the bulk of the book? The answer came quickly. Stories. The book would provide a rich treasury of stories from the Chinese opera. The organization was there in front of us. There! Were there not a number of plays about emperors in that corner of the table? And over here! Look at the number of ghost plays on this side. Shuffling the pictures around provided a number of categories that took us through a sort of Chinese chain of being from heaven, through the whole social structure on earth from emperor to outlaw, to ghosts in the nether world. Each of the remaining chapters would deal with stories centring on a particular link in the chain. Each would open with a dramatic photograph to illustrate the general theme, and would follow with the sights and stories of several characteristic operas.

It was an intriguing idea. Use stories from Chinese opera to provide a window on Chinese social structure and experience. It would also prove challenging. My immediate task was to find Chinese scripts of these plays. Some of the plays were famous, but I could not assume that the regional form shown in the photographs retold the story in the most familiar way. In fact, many well-known stories have telling variations in different opera styles. Thus a regional operatic version might have significant differences from the time-honoured folk story or from the Peking opera version. Other stories were not so well known, and we had little information for them beyond maddeningly short and vague program notes. Clearly, this project would require a great deal of research. Kate Stevens, in her meticulous way, had already organized a great deal of the information before I came to the project. Siu managed to locate some scripts in Hong Kong and mainland China. In addition, I was able to discover and verify information with the help of former professionals in regional opera who now live in Canada. A trip to Taiwan and Hong Kong to research and write was also instrumental to completion of the book.

The second task was to read the plays and retell them in a concise yet lively manner. That recounting also needed to provide useful comments to help the reader enter into the spirit of the story. Each section of the chain of being in the book begins with a short preface outlining traditional Chinese attitudes to that group. As romanized Chinese names can be confusing, naming characters has been done as little as possible. Pinyin romanization is used for names when they do appear and for the specialized terminology that appears in the chapters on regional opera styles and conventions. The only exceptions are for generally accepted names like Peking opera, instead of Beijing opera, and Cantonese opera, instead of Yue opera. (Indeed, there is an entirely different Yue opera style dealt with in this book, which is popular in Shanghai). The text refers to cities by their modern names.

This book is meant for many people. Devotees of the theatre, east or west, will find Siu Wang-Ngai's photographs a delight. They make the Chinese approach to drama concrete and vivid. The accompanying text gives these readers further access to this performance tradition by explaining the dramatic conventions and the stories. Those with a passion for China can use the photographs and text as an entry into traditional Chinese society, which still lives on the opera stage. The plays and commentary give them an intimate look at the lives of emperors, scholars, generals, common folk, and outlaws. Finally, this book is meant for all those who enjoy a good story. Chinese opera has a rich repertoire drawn from history, legends, myths, folk tales, and classic novels. These stories are full of colourful characters and surprising turns. It is not necessary to be interested in the Chinese dramatic tradition to sit back, like the Chinese audience of a regional opera, and enjoy a good yarn. Siu Wang-Ngai's record of regional opera performance makes these yarns come alive.

Acknowledgments

Siu Wang-Ngai

IN 1981 I WAS INVITED to watch a Cantonese opera, *The Jade Bracelet,* in which a friend of mine performed the role of Sun Yujiao. I happened to have a camera with me and took a series of pictures during the performance. The photo on page 153 in this book is from that series, and is a memorable image.

Nobody at that time had successfully attempted to photograph these operas in performance, as far as I knew. I was then looking for a theme to use in an attempt to gain a fellowship in the Royal Photographic Society, and this seemed tailor made. So I went, as a member of the audience, with cameras, to the Chinese theatre whenever an opera was performed. I grasped the technique as I progressed and gained experience.

In 1985, I got an RPS fellowship with this kind of photography. My interest continued to develop, not only as a photographer but also gradually as an opera lover. The opera styles I came across were then limited to Cantonese and Peking operas, but my chance came in 1986, when many regional opera troupes came to Hong Kong. I watched and took pictures of almost all the performances.

At the same time, however, I began to consider that people had become more practical; the career of an opera performer did not have a promising future. If performers found more lucrative jobs elsewhere, most would march away from the profession. After twenty or thirty years, we might be able to see performances only rarely, and the names of the opera styles, stories, and performers would only be found in books. I enjoy these performances and the characters in them; I admire the performers. The only way that I could ensure their preservation was to keep records in a lively and vivid way, in a series of colourful photos.

From 1986 until 1993, there was an annual Chinese regional opera festival, to which many troupes were invited. I attended the theatre constantly, taking more than 30,000 photos. In 1989 in Hong Kong, and again in 1992 in Vancouver, I displayed no fewer than 100 Chinese theatrical photos. But from 1994 to the present, operas have been performed less and less often. Some of the performers have died, retired, or changed their careers. A new generation must be brought up, encouraged, and trained, or this art will be seen no more after, say, fifty years. If my fear proves true, these photographs, if still preserved, will have some value and interest.

For their part in bringing *Chinese Opera* to print, I want to give my special thanks to the following people:

Kwan Lihuen, who had the vision, dedication, and perseverance to make this book happen.

Professor Kate Stevens, retired from the Department of East Asian Studies at the University of Toronto, who did so much preliminary research and organization and who poured boundless enthusiasm into the project.

R. Peter Milroy, Director of UBC Press, who supported and delighted in this endeavour.

The late Professor Leon Hurvitz.

Dr. Jan Walls, Director of the David Lam Centre for International Communications.

Paul Yeung Yu-Ping, chief executive of the Hong Kong Ballet.

He Saifei, Yang Nan, April Y.L. Lee, Claude Tsang Ka-Kit, and Chow Ka-Yee, who in various ways have made contributions to the production of this book.

The dramatist Shen Zu'an, who provided scripts for many of the plays in this book.

Special thanks to Camilla Jenkins. A good editor is a precious commodity and Camilla is a superb one. Her intelligent questions and meticulous editing have been of immense value.

Dynasties of China

Xia	ca. 2200 BC - ca. 1767 BC
Shang	ca. 1767 BC - ca. 1030 BC
Zhou	ca. 1030 BC - ca. 221 BC
Qin	221 BC - 206 BC
Han	206 BC - AD 220
Three Kingdoms	220-65
Southern and Northern	265-581
Sui	581-618
Tang	618-907
Five Dynasties	907-60
Northern Song	960-1127
Southern Song	1127-1279
Yuan	1279-1368
Ming	1368-1644
Qing	1644-1911
Republican China	1911-49
People's Republic of China	1949-

Note on Romanization

CHINESE WORDS IN THIS BOOK are romanized using the Pinyin system. The examples used here approximate standard Canadian pronunciation.

Initial Consonants

Initial consonants in the Pinyin romanization system are generally pronounced as they are in English with a few exceptions.

C is pronounced *ts* as in accep*ts*. *Cao Cao* is thus *tsao tsao*.
Q is pronounced *ch* as in *ch*urch. *Qing* is thus *ching*.
X is pronounced *hs* as in hal*cy*on. *Xia* is thus *hsia*.
Z is pronounced *dz* as in be*ds*. *Zeng* is thus *dzeng*.
Zh is pronounced *j* as in *j*udge. *Zhou* is thus *Joe*.

Vowels Following Initial Consonants

When an *i* follows *j, q,* or *x*, it is pronounced *ee*. *Ji* is thus *jee* as in *jeep*. *Qi* is *chee* as in *cheap*.
When an *i* follows *zh, ch,* or *sh*, it is pronounced *irr*. *Zhi* is thus *jour* as in *jour*ney. *Chi* is *chir* as in *chir*p. *Shi* is *shir* as in *shir*k.
When an *i* follows *z, c,* or *s*, the sound can only be approximated in English. The vowel is similar to that in the second syllable of *mussel*, if the final *l* is omitted.
When a *u* follows *j, q,* or *x*, it is pronounced as with an umlaut. *Ju* is thus *jü*, a sound not found in English. *Qu* is *chü*.
When a *u* follows *zh, ch, sh, r, z, c,* or *s*, it is pronounced *oo*. *Zhu* is thus *ju* as in *ju*ice. *Chu* is *choo* as in *choo*se.

Finals

Finals are vowels and consonants at the end of words.

A is *ah* as in *baa baa* (black sheep). *Sa* is thus *sah*.
Ai is *ah-ee* as in *lie*. *Lai* is thus *lie*.
An is *ahn* as in H*ans*. *Lan* is thus *lahn*.

Ang is *ahng* as in long. *Wang* is thus *Wahng.*
Ao is *ow* as in cow. *Hao* is thus *how.*
Ei is *ay* as in eight. *Gei* is thus *gay.*
En is *uhn* as in gun. *Ben* is thus *bun.*
Eng is *uhng* as in sung. *Geng* is thus *guhng.*
Ia is *eeya* as in Asia. *Jia* is thus *jeeya.*
Ian is *eeyen* as in yen. *Jian* is thus *jeeyen.*
Iang is *eeyahng. Liang* is thus *leeyahng.*
Iao is *eeow* as in meeow. *Liao* is thus *leeow.*
Ie is *ee-eh* as in yesterday. *Lie* is thus *lee-eh.*
In is *in* as in kin. *Qin* is thus *chin.*
Ing is *ing* as in wing. *Xing* is thus *hsing.*
Iong is *eeoong* as in Jung. *Xiong* is thus *hseeoong.*
Iu is *ee-o* as in yo-yo. *Jiu* is thus *jeeo.*
Ou is *o* as in cold. *Gou* is thus *go.*
Ong is *oong* as in Jung. *Song* is thus *soong.*
U is *u* as in crude. *Qu* is thus *choo.*
Ua is *oo-ah* as in water. *Hua* is thus *hooah.*
Uai is *oo-ai* as in while. *Huai* is thus *hooai.*
Uan is *ooahn* as in Juan. *Guan* is thus *gooahn.*
Uang is *ooahng. Huang* is thus *hooahng.*

Chinese Opera

Chapter 1

The Dramatic Tradition

CACOPHONY! Cymbals, gongs, and drum demand attention. Their incessant beating fills up every corner of the theatre. Their rhythm and pace are urgent and exciting, as if to say, 'This is important! Something is about to happen!' The musicians sitting on stage left in clear view of the audience are intensely focused on their leader, who furiously beats a small drum on a tripod with two sticks. The stage itself is fully lit but bare except for a carpet.

Suddenly a whirlwind of colour blows in from stage right, quickly followed by another. Fantastic beings, made larger than life by enormous shoes and padded shoulders, leap before the audience. They wear heavy, gloriously embroidered costumes and hold tasselled whips out at their sides, making them undulate. Four pennants rise from each of their backs and flutter as they move. But the most astonishing thing about them is their faces, painted in bold and calculated designs of many colours. Everything gives the impression that some mythical creatures have taken the stage. Then one of them begins to sing. A powerful and arresting voice resonates nasally. The delivery is aimed directly at the audience.

A first visit to the Chinese opera is an overwhelming experience of colour, sound, and movement. The dramatic tradition of China is a blend of song, speech, mime, dance, and acrobatics, held together by theatrical conventions resting on a concept of drama quite different from the realism and naturalism that have had such influence in the West. A realist play re-creates a story on stage down to the smallest detail. The characters are unaware of the audience; actors are trained to believe in the situation so that the audience will too. The Chinese tradition, however, presents rather than reproduces the story. Waving a tasselled whip indicates riding a horse, and letting it hang straight down from the finger-tips shows that the rider has dismounted. There is no need to bring a live animal on stage to convey the idea of a horse. The stage is bare to give the actors the imaginative flexibility they need to suggest what is happening. Walking in a circle around the stage, for example, conveys making a long journey. When they arrive at the end of their journey, they may use mime to open an imaginary door and step over an imaginary ledge into a house. A table and two chairs can become a mountain from which a general surveys the battlefield. Acrobatics indicate the war.

These stage conventions make the performance accessible. The audience also

1.1
The imperial kinsmen, in The Imperial Kinsmen.
Longjiang opera

finds clarity in the make-up and costumes of the actors. It knows when it sees a man in oily white make-up that he is crafty and not to be trusted, just as a man in red make-up is courageous and generous. The inner hearts of these characters are painted on their faces, as are their specific identities. The audience sees a given facial design on an actor and knows immediately that he is portraying this particular general or that particular legendary being. Costume reveals the character's social station. An actress appears in a red and gold embroidered gown with tasselled cape and an elaborate headdress. The audience instantly understands that she is playing an imperial concubine. Thus an audience can size up characters pretty well before they have uttered a word. But then they do speak or sing, addressing the audience directly and giving a synopsis of who they are, what has happened to them, and why they are here now. Once characters have performed this introduction, they are then free to engage others as the scene progresses.

Musical styles and stories vary among the many regional operas of China, but conventions are generally shared. They use accepted and familiar methods of demonstrating how something occurred. The audience delights in watching how well these are executed. Much like the audience of a traditional Western opera, Chinese opera-goers know the story very well before it begins. They are there to enjoy the execution of a particular aria, acrobatic scene, or much-loved part of a story. Right into the twentieth century, people would come into a teahouse or theatre in the middle of a performance and chat or eat, waiting for favourite spots.

This approach to the theatre goes back century upon century. When Chinese drama begins depends on how you define it. It is crucial to keep in mind that drama in China is a synthesis of many arts, and tracing the development of the one means tracing the development of the many. A good example is an exorcism performed in Taiwan in 1982. An elderly woman was afflicted by devils. The Taoist priest arrived on the scene in ceremonial robes to do what was necessary to free her. He breathed fire and had a battle of wits with the demon, played by a masked assistant. He spoke, he sang, he gestured. The battle with the infernal reached its climax with acrobatics and dance that went on far into the night. There was great drama and great seriousness in this event. Priests in the second millennium BC used dance in ritual with the same seriousness. Oracle bones – the shoulders of oxen or the shells of turtles, inscribed with divinations – tell of Shang dynasty priests performing rain dances. These shamans used ritual dance as well in spiritual communion and in exorcism.

Dance in later dynasties performed the function of memory. *The Great Warrior Dance*, called *Dawu* in Chinese, re-enacted how the King of Zhou overthrew the Shang in 1030 BC. Lines of court dancers imitating a battle performed *Dawu* and kept an important event alive and present. A later dance in the Tang dynasty (AD 618-907) told the story of Prince Lanling, who was so good-looking that his enemies would not take him seriously in battle. His wife made him ferocious masks to solve the problem. This performance gives us an example of combined dramatic elements – a dance that told a story and employed masks – and the tale of Prince Lanling is still alive on the Chinese operatic stage. Another dance from the same period was *The Stepping and Swaying Lady.* A woman walked and swayed on stage lamenting her sad fate: her husband abused her when he was drunk. A chorus sympathetically joined in, but then her husband entered, his nose red from drunkenness, and they fought. The elements of drama are all here: music, singing, movement, a situation, characters, and even, as the red nose suggests, make-up.[1]

Another example of the meeting of dramatic elements comes in the person of the court fool. The Zhou kings counted jesters among their entertainers. Like the Elizabethan fool, the Chinese court jester performed comedy and had a certain licence to speak more frankly than others. The name of one of them, Jester Meng, figures in the development of Chinese drama. One day, the story goes, Jester Meng encountered a young man cutting and selling wood to stay alive. This man, it turned out, was the son of the late prime minister, who had served his king honestly and well. Now that the prime minister was dead, however, his son was reduced to poverty. The jester promised to help and then proceeded to spend an entire year preparing the role of the deceased official. He practised his mannerisms, walk, and appearance. When ready, Jester Meng performed the role at a banquet before the amazed king and appealed to his conscience. Apparently, it worked.[2]

The fool turns into one of the first definite role types in Chinese dramatic history, and that is another story. Around the third century AD, a high-ranking minister stole some silk from his king. He was found out and his punishment was to be a terrible one – humiliation. He had to dress up at banquets, presumably in the silk that he stole, and play the butt of the court fool's slapstick jokes. This quickly became a successful entertainment known as adjutant drama, either because the official was an adjutant or because one fool performed so well that he was awarded adjutant status. By the beginning of the Song dynasty (AD 960-1279), the adjutant drama had expanded to five set roles, becoming something new – an entertainment in the form of a play. The adjutant had become a character type called a *fujing,* and the character who made the adjutant the butt of jokes had become the *fumo.* Three other roles – a woman, a man, and an official – were added, though they were subordinate to the other two.[3]

Role types are a distinctive feature of the Chinese opera and another way in which the action is clarified for the audience. Characters are grouped by four main types: the female, the male, the clown, and the painted face. Each type has further subgroups. Chinese actors specialize in a role type depending on body and voice. Scripts refer to the role type in addition to or in place of a character's name. Each type has its way of singing, talking, and moving, its own prescribed make-up and

1 This subject is discussed fully in Wang Kefan, *The History of Chinese Dance* (Beijing: Foreign Languages Press 1985).

2 See William Dolby's 'Early Chinese Plays and Theatre' in *Chinese Theater,* ed. Colin Mackerras (Honolulu: University of Hawaii Press 1983).

3 See the treatment of farce in Colin Mackerras, *Chinese Drama: A Historical Approach* (Beijing: New World Press 1990).

costumes. Role type underscores the centrality of the actor, who conveys much of what scenery and props impart in other theatrical systems. These characteristics, common to many regional operas, were evident in the Song troupes of over 1,000 years ago.

The Song troupes began performing something called variety drama, or *zaju*, a program of entertainment that involved separate items of dance, music, acrobatics, and impersonation centred on short farces. These farces were high slapstick, a popular entertainment full of joking. Italy has its *commedia dell'arte*, with Columbine, Harlequin, and the great joke of the *lazzi*, the interpolated comic business. China has its Song *zaju*, with the *fumo*, the *fujing*, and hilarious slapstick. These farce programs were performed in entertainment districts, which by the time of the Song dynasty were established in major cities. Accounts from the time tell us that the capital city had over fifty theatres in three major entertainment districts, and that each theatre could accommodate well over a thousand people.

What was going on in these *washe*, as the entertainment districts were known? Aside from variety drama, an audience could enjoy puppetry, storytelling, and all kinds of acrobatic performance collectively called 'the hundred games.' Fire breathing, balancing acts, and stilt walking all competed for attention. One of the forerunners of the hundred games was an entertainment called horn butting. It was a dramatic form of wrestling that grew out of an ancient legend. In prehistory a king of the south attacked the great Yellow Emperor of the north. The southern enemy and his many kinsmen were fierce fighters. They wore horns on their heads like Vikings and butted people with them. The legend gave birth to horn-butting entertainment: wrestling or fighting in costume and within some context. The story *Huang of the Eastern Sea*, for example, employed stage fighting. Huang was a great fighter who hedged his bets with magic to overcome tigers. He was a striking figure in his crimson headband and waving a golden sword, but as time passed and age overtook him he indulged in wine so much that his magic began to ebb away. Yet Huang still set out to challenge the dreaded white tiger. He lost. The dramatic elements in this little scenario include costume, prop, conflict, and action. So it was that by the time of the Song the various elements that now make up Chinese opera were rubbing shoulders in the entertainment districts.[4] Performers and writers wanted to push beyond a simple situation or farce.

Southern drama, or *nanxi*, was performed about AD 1120 in the southeastern coastal city of Wenzhou. In this genre, several role types sang and spoke in an extended play. A story was developed over numerous scenes reaching a climax and resolution. Although there are 238 recorded *nanxi* titles, only five scripts survive. One of them, *The Magistrate's Son Chooses the Wrong Career*, tells a great deal about early Chinese theatre. The local magistrate's son falls in love with an actress. His father is furious that the son spends his time on frivolous activities such as

4 Acrobatics and games are thoroughly discussed in Fu Qifeng, *Chinese Acrobatics through the Ages* (Beijing: Foreign Languages Press 1985).

theatre and with low-class people like actresses, and so forbids him to go out. In defiance, the son runs away to be an actor so that he might accompany his beloved. She belongs to a travelling family acting company. They go from town to town, festival to festival, theatre to theatre, and perform where they can. The actress's father is as unwilling to accept the magistrate's son as the magistrate was unwilling to accept the actress. Can the boy dance? Can he do acrobatics? What about music and recitation? How well does he know the farce scripts? Will he be able to manage the drums and the costumes? The magistrate's son promises that he can. He is made for make-up! The talents that the young man must display in order to join the company show the breadth of the actor's talent and the demands made by plays.[5] The synthesis of arts in Chinese drama stands out clearly in this single theatrical form, but there were also other forms.

Northern drama, called Yuan *zaju*, was a sophisticated theatrical achievement that gained prominence in the thirteenth century. China had been invaded by the Mongolians. The Song dynasty was driven south for a time but eventually capitulated. The new regime, calling itself the Yuan dynasty, was deeply suspicious of the conquered Han Chinese, who were Song loyalists, and of Confucian scholars in particular. It preferred to put foreigners, such as Marco Polo, in authority. Foreigners were likely to be grateful, unattached to the fallen Song, and not predisposed to conspiracy. Some of the now unoccupied Han Chinese scholars in the north turned to play writing, producing works of a higher literary quality than the southern drama. Many of the plays concerned love and many others concerned injustice. One of the great moving forces in Yuan *zaju* was the scholar Guan Hanqing, who wrote over fifty plays and is still celebrated as one of China's greatest dramatists.[6]

The success of northern drama was largely in the writing. Tightly plotted stories were executed through a precise, demanding, and beautiful format. The plays presented their stories in four short acts. Some dramatists also used a short expository scene, called a wedge, which could appear before an act when needed. Only one character could sing per act, but the singing character could change from act to act. The other characters spoke in prose and poetry. All the songs in an act used the same key and the dramatists had to be mindful of strict rhyming schemes. The music has not survived, but we know that it used the Chinese lute, drum, gong, and wooden clappers.

Yuan *zaju* used mime, make-up, costume, role types, in fact all the ingredients that came together in southern drama. This new drama spread from north to south, and actresses made great reputations for themselves. The Yuan dynasty, however, was short-lived. The Mongolians were driven out and replaced by a Han Chinese dynasty – the Ming – from the south in 1368. With its arrival came another development in the Chinese theatrical tradition.

Members of the Ming royal house were great patrons of the theatre, and some of

5 'Grandee's Son Takes the Wrong Career,' in *Eight Chinese Plays,* ed. William Dolby (New York: Columbia University Press 1978).

6 For a discussion of Guan Hanqing and an authoritative treatment of Yuan drama, see J.I. Crump, *Chinese Theatre in the Days of Kublai Khan* (Tucson: University of Arizona Press 1980).

7 Gao Ming, *The Lute,* trans. Jean Mulligan (New York: Columbia University Press 1980).

the princes wrote plays themselves. The first Ming emperor was particularly fond of a dramatic piece in forty-two scenes written by the scholar Gao Ming. It was called *The Lute.*[7] Gao Ming's play tells the story of a poor scholar, Cai Bojie, who obeys his parents and leaves his wife in order to go to the capital to write the civil service exams. He distinguishes himself so much that the emperor detains him for years and arranges his marriage to the prime minister's daughter. Meanwhile, famine has hit the countryside. Scholar Cai Bojie's parents are starving, and his first wife, Zhao Wuniang, undergoes all kinds of hardship to serve them as a dutiful daughter-in-law. She is finally reduced to surviving on rice husks as her only food. Cai Bojie's parents die, and Zhao Wuniang, penniless, cuts and sells her hair to raise money for their burial. She carries mud and earth in her clothes to build them a tomb. Having buried them, Zhao Wuniang now makes for the capital playing the lute and singing as she goes to beg for handouts. There is a tearful reunion, and Cai Bojie's second wife is deeply moved by Zhao Wuniang's devotion and suffering. All three return to live in a hut by the graves and mourn for three years. The play ends with imperial commendation for all three for their filiality.

The Ming emperor liked this play so much that he ordered back to back performances and had his music academy compose a string accompaniment. *The Lute* was a new kind of play. It did not follow the strict discipline of Yuan *zaju.* It was southern and had a southern temperament. Like the *nanxi,* it told a story through many scenes, and different characters could sing solo or together. *The Lute* was distinct, however, in that it took those characteristics to perfection. The writing was particularly fine, the songs exquisitely beautiful. It was the work of a cultivated mind, and a single performance took days to complete.

This new dramatic form was known as *chuanqi,* and it became the dominant drama and art form of the literati. The plays quoted from master poets, presented erudite debate, and used rich language to draw beautiful landscapes. The playwright is very much present in these dramas.

The music of the early *chuanqi* has not survived, but music later devised to be worthy of these complex dramas has. In the middle of the sixteenth century, the musical scholar and singer Wei Liangfu devoted ten years to develop a new musical style. He used his experience and knowledge of local singing styles to produce 'water-polishing music.' It was so beautiful, refined, and smooth that listeners compared it to running water polishing a stone. Gentle flute music was one of its main characteristics. Styles of music in China were called by the names of the locales to which they were attached. As Wei Liangfu had settled in the southeastern town of Kunshan, his water-polishing music was also called *kunshan* music. It was successfully applied to a *chuanqi* play entitled *Washing Silk* in 1579. *Kunshan* music was made for the *chuanqi.* Its delicate, languorous quality was the perfect vehicle for the poetry and high literary standards of that drama. One became identified with the other so that *chuanqi* plays were now referred to as *kunqu* – dramas in the *kunshan* musical style.

Kunqu was the dominant dramatic form for the next 200 years. Talented dramatists produced enduring plays throughout its development. One of the most famous writers was Tang Xianzu, who wrote four plays. His masterpiece is *The Peony Pavilion*. It is a love story of two young people who meet in a dream and overcome the obstacles of this world and the next to be together. A later southern playwright was Hong Sheng. His *Palace of Eternal Youth* tells the story of Emperor Ming, who neglects the nation in his devotion to the beautiful concubine Yang, commonly known as Yang Guifei. His devotion reaches even beyond the grave. Kong Shangren, a northern playwright and contemporary of Hong Sheng, wrote *Peach Blossom Fan*. That play is a story of love and separation set against the fall of the Ming dynasty in 1644. These plays are classic *kunqu* performances. Particularly loved excerpts are still performed on the Chinese stage.[8]

The Ming dynasty fell, and a new one rose. The new Qing dynasty was from Manchuria, in the north. During this last imperial dynasty, *kunqu* lost its premier place among the performing arts to a new arrival, the Peking opera. The key event was the birthday of the Qing emperor in 1790, which provided an occasion for regional troupes to go to the capital, Beijing.

 Four theatre companies from the southeastern province of Anhui arrived for the birthday party and brought with them new styles of music called *erhuang* and *xipi*. These four companies and their music became the pre-eminent theatrical force in the capital throughout the nineteenth century. The theatre that developed there over time became identified with the capital city and so today is known as the Peking opera.

By the time of the Qing emperor's birthday, regional theatre styles had already established their popularity. They were generally more vigorous and more accessible than the highly literate *kunqu,* which was already somewhat in decline. One regional style, clapper opera, had made a name for itself in the capital by 1779. It was called clapper because one of its chief characteristics was the sound of a stick striking datewood. A clapper opera actor named Wei Changsheng became famous for his impersonation of women.[9] He devised a walk on specially contrived shoes that imitated a woman's bound feet. His coiffure became the standard for female roles. Women's roles are now generally played by actresses on the opera stage, but the performance style of the role type developed through the work of female impersonators.

Female impersonators were the stars through the early nineteenth century, but this had changed by mid-century. The old man's role – a subcategory of the male role – began to come into its own. Just as the development of female roles is associated with Wei Changsheng, so the old man's role is connected with actor Cheng

8 See Hsu Tao-Ching, *The Chinese Conception of the Theatre* (Seattle: University of Washington Press 1985), 272ff.

9 See Part 1 of Colin Mackerras, *The Chinese Theatre in Modern Times* (London: Thames and Hudson 1975) for an overview of the development of the Peking opera.

Changgeng, who was the head of one of the four Anhui companies that settled in Beijing. His voice was legendary. Cheng Changgeng preferred historical, patriotic dramas to the love stories in which female roles had made their mark. His singing style, refinements of *erhuang* music, and preference for a particular type of drama spread beyond his company to influence the evolving new dramatic style.

By the twentieth century, Peking opera had become the first among China's dramatic forms. It has even been referred to as the national opera. This term can be misleading if it suggests that there is an audience for Peking opera everywhere in China. The most popular operatic form in any one part of China is its own regional opera. But the Peking opera does have a special place in that it is centred in the capital, has gained worldwide exposure, and has distilled the best of other forms.

The twentieth century has been a time of change, revolution, and experiment for China. It has been so for drama as well. Spoken drama – a genre following Western realism and naturalism, particularly Ibsen – appeared in 1919. New regional performance styles emerged. The Peking opera made various reforms, among them using scenery and experimenting with instrumentation. One of China's greatest actors, Mei Lanfang, who specialized in women's roles, made significant and lasting changes to the costumes, make-up, staging, and texts of the operas.

Despite these modifications, traditional opera came under attack in the early 1960s, when former film actress Jiang Qing, Chairman Mao's wife, accused it of not serving the needs of the masses. She decried the constant presentation of emperors, beauties, and the wealthy gentry of a feudal, Confucianist time. Madam Mao promoted a revolution in opera that became one of the distinctive features of China's decade-long cultural revolution. It was led by the now infamous Gang of Four, which was later vilified for usurping power and ruining the country.[10] During the cultural revolution, no traditional opera was performed. Eight models were held up instead, with names like *Taking Tiger Mountain by Strategy* and *The Red Lantern*. They incorporated some Chinese operatic traditions such as music, singing style, acrobatics, and certain stage conventions like using a horse whip to stand for the horse. They eliminated, or updated, many others. Traditional costumes were replaced by modern dress. The fantastic make-up of the painted-face character was dropped. More naturalistic sets and props were used. One could see, then, a character in modern dress ride on stage using mime and a horse whip and then shooting off a pistol. These operas were photographed, filmed, written as novels and comic books, broadcast, and taken on tour to the West.

After the Gang of Four fell, traditional opera quickly made a comeback, but it has sustained considerable damage. An entire generation has lost an orientation and upbringing in a theatrical form that was once popular and close to the people. Younger audiences, in the main, opt for film and Western-style entertainments,

10 See the Introduction to Constantine Tung and Colin Mackerras, *Drama in the People's Republic of China* (Albany: State University of New York Press 1987).

which do not require the kind of familiarity with story, stage conventions, and musical forms that traditional opera does.

Experimentation in dramatic form continues, however, and is reflected in the plays in this collection. The challenge is to continue an exquisite tradition in a lively way and to regain a lost audience. Chinese opera must avoid fossilization yet at the same time maintain the thread that gives it its identity.

A first visit to the Chinese opera is an overwhelming experience. It gives the spectator matchless excitement in the surprise of its execution. It is simply beautiful to watch. Any effort to understand the conventions and background of this performance art is rewarded many times over by the deeper access it gives to the theatrical experience of the Chinese stage.

HEILONGJIANG

JILIN

LIAONING

XINJIANG

INNER
MONGOLIA

Beijing
(Peking) • • Tangshan

• Tianjin

HEBEI

SHANXI

SHANDONG

NINGXIA

QINGHAI

Yellow
Sea

GANSU

Xi'an
(Chang'an) •

JIANGSU

HENAN

Yangzhou

Nanjing • • Kunshan

SHAANXI

ANHUI Suzhou • • Shanghai
Haiyan

HUBEI Anqing • Hangzhou • Yuyao Shaoxing

SICHUAN

Yangtze

Chengdu •

ZHEJIANG

East Chin

Yiyang •

Sea

JIANGXI

HUNAN

FUJIAN

Wenzhou

GUIZHOU

Gan

GUANGXI

GUANGDONG

Guangzhou
(Canton)

YUNNAN

Foshan •

Bay
of
Bengal

South China

Sea

Heilong

Chapter 2   Regional Opera Styles

1 See the bibliography of Chinese materials at the end of the book for excellent Chinese-language sources on regional opera styles.

THE PEKING OPERA that emerged from China's dramatic tradition gained special status because it was so closely connected with the capital and patronized by the court. It also combined the best of several different opera styles. Peking opera repertoire was largely concerned with historical or legendary stories that emphasized virtue, courage, and loyalty. Thus it had a patriotic element and consequently spread throughout China, becoming much more than just a local theatre. In the West, the Peking opera has come to represent the Chinese approach to theatre. Local Peking amateur groups, visits from Chinese Peking opera companies, and scholarly work on Chinese drama have emphasized this impression.

There are, however, more than 300 different regional opera styles in China.[1] They have emerged from rice-planting dances, tea-picking songs, storytelling modes, and cross-pollenization with other opera styles. They have much in common, including the focus on role types. The female, male, painted-face, and clown roles, each with its own subdivisions, are standard. The expressive performance style is executed in varying degrees of formality. Singing, gesture, dialogue, poetry, and dance constitute the delivery. Although there are variations in costume and make-up, these, too, carry across regional styles. And in all the regions, emphasis is generally given to costume rather than to scenery or props, making Chinese theatre truly portable. The operas often share the same stories as well, although the versions might have different endings, additional characters, and so on. This book therefore specifies which version of a given story is being related.

The main distinctions from one opera form to another are found in the music and dialect; local music and speech give the operas their particular regional identity. One style is melodic and gentle; another is fast paced and powerful. One uses mostly strings; another uses flutes.

The regional operas can be classified roughly into four main categories according to the main musical style with which they are associated. The first is 'high music,' or *gaoqiang*, a term referring to a number of singing styles that can all be traced back to a southeastern percussive style called *yiyang*. High music is believed to get its name from the very high, forceful falsetto in which it is sung, or possibly because of its popularity in Gaoyang district. The second is clapper music from the northwest, which is characterized by the sound of a stick hitting a datewood block.

It is accompanied by strings, primarily the moon guitar. Although its early development is poorly documented, it probably came from Shaanxi province. Clapper music was well established by the middle of the eighteenth century. The third is the *pihuang* musical system, a combination of two distinct melodies from southeastern China. *Pihuang* became the major theatrical operatic style, and is used by the Peking opera. The fourth is folk music, particularly the rice-planting and tea-picking songs that are at the root of so many regional styles.

Siu Wang-Ngai's photographs cover a number of different regional opera styles. Some have histories going back several hundred years, while others have emerged in this century. What follows are descriptions of the various opera styles found in this book, organized geographically more or less from north to south. While the styles often bear the name of the region or province in which they developed, the size of Chinese provinces and the geographical barriers within them have prompted the development of different dialects and musical styles within the same province.

Longjiang Opera
龍江劇

Heilongjiang is China's most northern province. It gets its name from the Heilong River, which means black dragon. The river winds like a twisting dragon from west to east to form China's northern border. The northeastern provinces are remote and not as developed as the southerly ones. The Chinese government decided in the 1950s to cultivate the development of regional drama there. Thus, opera that comes from this region is a very recent addition to the Chinese stage, getting its name in 1960.

It is based on a traditional storytelling form called 'two-person turnabout,' which can be performed in a number of ways. One of the most common involves a woman and a clown who sing, speak, and dance in a short and lively comedic skit. They are accompanied by the wooden fiddle, the *suona*, or Chinese oboe, and the hand-held wooden clapper, similar to castanets. The two-person turnabout grew out of rice-planting songs and is related to the 'falling lotus' storytelling style and the *bengbeng* folk dance in Hebei province (see Ping opera). The Longjiang opera expanded the two-person turnabout and incorporated northeastern folk music for an opera form that emphasizes dance and gesture and possesses a strong local identity. The music is generally high spirited and forceful but can also become sentimental. Performance technique and stage design are abstract and symbolic. Thus actors perform in a broad and expressive manner against simple but beautiful backgrounds. By the late 1960s, this new regional drama had already produced more than seventy representative operas. They include both civil and military plays, the latter involving acrobatics and martial arts. The operas draw on historical events and legends like those from *The Romance of the Three Kingdoms* and well-known stories like *Dream of the Red Chamber*.

Heilongjiang province

Hebei province

Hebei Clapper Opera
河北梆子戲

Hebei province is the site of China's capital, Beijing. It means 'north of the river' and gets its name from its location north of the vital Yellow River, around which Chinese civilization first arose. The main operatic form is clapper music. Hebei Clapper opera goes back to the beginning of the nineteenth century. At that time, there was a shift away from the highly refined, extremely literate southern opera, *kunqu,* to the more lively *yiyang* style from the south and to clapper music from the adjacent provinces of Shaanxi and Shanxi. The clapper style spread from the villages to China's great cities like Beijing, Shanghai, and Tianjin to become a powerful theatrical influence.

Singers of the musical style popular in Beijing – called *jingqiang,* or 'capital style' – began to perform clapper melodies, giving them a unique flavour. These artists introduced melodic and tonal innovations based on their own experience and designed to suit the tastes of local audiences. By 1850 a clapper opera had arisen in Beijing that was distinct from its predecessor in Shaanxi and Shanxi. By 1900 it had become the major theatrical force in the province and the main competitor with Peking opera in the capital.

Hebei Clapper opera is more accessible to regional audiences than is the classic *kunqu* because it is easier to understand and uses many northern expressions. The singing is energetic, high, and bright, accompanied by the clear rhythm of clapper music. The main instrument is the wood-faced fiddle; unlike other Chinese fiddles it has a wooden rather than a snakeskin sound box.

Traditional Hebei Clapper opera comes from the Shaanxi-Shanxi clapper tradition. Once in Beijing, however, Hebei Clapper opera troupes began performing stories taken from the Peking opera. The Peking opera, in turn, adapted clapper stories into its repertoire. The heyday of Hebei Clapper opera was from 1870 to 1920, when it drew large audiences with plays focusing on the female role, usually, but not exclusively, played by men. The other role types were consequently downplayed, leading to a general decline in performance standards for them. Tastes changed and the clapper troupes began to lose popularity. With the Japanese invasion of northern China in the early 1930s, Hebei clapper artists dispersed. Clapper troupes have reconstituted themselves, however, and once again hold their place as an important branch of Chinese regional opera.

Ping Opera
評劇

Ping opera is popular theatre that evolved around the mining town of Tangshan in Hebei province from a local storytelling style and a folk dance. The storytelling form was called 'falling lotus' and used seven-piece castanets – seven short pieces of bamboo strung in a row and alternating with coins – to provide a rhythmic accompaniment to a seated storyteller. By the end of the Qing dynasty, these stories were told by six seated but costumed performers who took role types. The most important roles were the male and female clowns. Many of these storyteller troupes were refugee families fleeing famine, drought, or flood with nothing to rely on but their familiarity with falling lotus. Independent performers also banded together to form falling lotus troupes.

The opera style that appeared in Tangshan around 1910 combined falling lotus storytelling with the popular music used in a Hebei folk dance called the *bengbeng*. *Beng* means 'jump' in the local dialect, and so *bengbeng* was an energetic leaping dance. The new Bengbeng opera was extremely popular with the miners there. They found it lively, contemporary, and accessible. One performer in particular, Cheng Zhaocai, gained a following and made a number of contributions to this new theatrical style. One was to replace the third-person narrative with the first-person voice of characters in the drama. Another was to adopt clapper and Peking opera rhythms, instrumentation, and singing styles to produce a fast-paced, powerful performance. The opera style was initially identified with Tangshan and thus known as Tangshan falling lotus. It also became closely identified with the nearby district of Yongping (today called Lulong), however, which, like Tangshan, took to it with great enthusiasm. It was eventually Yongping that gave the form its name: Ping opera.

Ideas from spoken Western-style drama had a strong influence on Ping opera. Like spoken drama, Ping opera focused on contemporary themes close to daily life. Formed in the country, the operas are rich in scenes from village life. The performance style is natural, and the singing is done in colloquial Mandarin with some Tangshan slang. Listening to a Ping opera performance, one can clearly hear the music shifting between Peking opera style and *bengbeng*. It is at once both lyrical and strongly rhythmic. Performers brought Ping opera to Beijing, Tianjin, and Shanghai. It gained popularity wherever it went. Talented and well-known dramatists who worked in the new 'spoken drama' form in Shanghai supported Ping opera by writing for it and arranging for it to be filmed. The most famous performers of this twentieth-century opera were women, but in recent years men have also gained popularity as Ping opera singers.

Jin Opera
晉劇

The northern province of Shanxi was part of the state of Jin in ancient times. One of Shanxi's regional operas has gone by various names throughout its development but is now known as Jin opera, taking its name from the ancient state. The Jin opera is a variant clapper style and one of four great clapper operas found in Shanxi. In other provinces it thus was called Shanxi Clapper opera or Central Shanxi

Shanxi province

16

Clapper opera, pointing to its origins in the province's central region, Puzhou. Its beginnings are not clear, but it is known that the early Shanxi Clapper in the Qing dynasty was performed entirely by artists from Puzhou. Performers from other parts of the province who wanted to learn this clapper form studied with Puzhou opera masters. Consequently, the local Puzhou dialect became its standard language. As the opera grew in popularity, it incorporated various rice-planting song styles. Professional Jin opera companies were in existence by the early twentieth century and followed Shanxi merchants to Hebei, Shaanxi, Gansu, and Inner Mongolia, gaining a wider audience.

Jin opera emphasizes the male, female, and painted-face roles, most often the first two. Interestingly, the male roles are often played by women. The famous actress Ding Guoxian, who performed in the 1920s and 1930s, was particularly well known for her portrayal of old men. Performance style tends to be broad and demonstrative. Jin opera stresses singing skills more than action or fighting skills. In addition to chorus singing, the Jin opera is known for its extended sung dialogue, which is generally fast and high pitched, with much use of the falsetto. The singing is accompanied by a nine-member orchestra divided into two sections: strings and winds; and percussion. Aside from the clapper, which sets the pace for the music, lead instruments are the fiddle, banjo, Chinese oboe, flute, and drums. In recent years, orchestration has included the Western violin, cello, brass, and woodwind instruments. Of about 400 traditional pieces that run the gamut from comic to tragic, approximately 200 plays are in performance repertoire.

Qin Opera
秦腔

Shaanxi province produced a regional drama that spread throughout China, making an immense impact on the development of opera wherever it went. The origins of this theatrical style are in traditional folk music, although it is not clear just how old the form is. It was already popular and spreading out of the province in the mid-sixteenth century. The opera uses clapper music and thus is sometimes called Guangguang opera, 'guang' being an imitation of the sound of the wooden clappers used in performance. The more common name is Qin opera, however, after the ancient state of Qin, which included modern-day Shaanxi.

The famous female impersonator, Wei Changsheng, was a key figure in the spread of Qin opera. He made several appearances in Beijing beginning in 1779, laying the groundwork for the yet-to-be-developed Peking opera. In addition to his appearances in Peking, he led opera troupes into provinces such as Zhejiang, Jiangxi, and Hunan.

Qin opera made its way down to Guangdong province in the south and up to Xinjiang in the northwest. By 1800, the form was established throughout China.

Shaanxi province

There were thirty-six Qin companies in the city of Xi'an alone. With performances in so many regions, local variants of the Qin opera began to emerge. These used the basic musical structure of clapper opera but incorporated local tunes and dialect. The term *luantan* – which simply means music that is neither *kunqu* nor high music – has become identified with clapper styles and often refers to Qin opera.

Qin opera music is generally high pitched and makes use of the falsetto. Its melodies are divided into two general categories: joyful and tragic. The music also uses decorative singing, which is an extended falsetto vocalization on the sound 'yi.' Singing is accompanied by rich string and wind orchestration involving various types of fiddles, the lute, the flute, and the *suona*. In recent years, orchestration has been expanded to include other Chinese instruments as well as Western instruments like the violin. A precursor and the main contributor to the development of the Peking opera, the Qin opera was in turn influenced in the twentieth century by the Peking opera and other dramas. Its strong, powerful delivery became softer; the broad gestures and expression of emotion became more precise. Qin opera repertoire is rich in historical drama, classical stories, and myths. There are over 2,700 performance pieces. Among these, stories from *The Romance of the Three Kingdoms* – legendary tales from the period of the Three Kingdoms dynasty – and about the Yang generals are the most frequently presented. There are thirteen role types: four male, six female, two painted faces, and a clown.

Sichuan Opera
川劇

Sichuan is a rich and productive province in western China. Until modern times, it had a reputation for being isolated and hard to reach. Difficult mountain trails connected it to the north, and rivers connected it to the southeast. Despite this isolation, Sichuan opera emerged by blending five regional styles. Only one, the lantern play, was local to Sichuan. The lantern play was folk theatre performed by peasants and village shamans at festivals. It got its name from the lanterns that lit the performance space at night. The plays were short and simple, requiring only three actors. Their predominant characteristic was spoken dialogue in the vernacular rather than singing. The dialogue was punctuated by music performed by two musicians using a small drum, a gong, and a fiddle.

The *yiyang* musical style from southeastern China – the second of the five influences and the style from which high music developed – reached Sichuan about the middle of the seventeenth century. The tunes were accompanied only by percussion. A notable feature of *yiyang*, and now a trademark of Sichuan opera, was the helping chorus. This chorus or choir sat in full view of the audience, singing a commentary on the action. It could also take over a character's singing part, leaving the actor to pantomime the movements.

Sichuan province

Northern clapper opera entered Sichuan sometime before the late eighteenth century, becoming the third influence on the provincial opera style. Clapper opera used a fuller orchestration than did high music and was regulated by constant beating on a wooden block.

Fiddle music from the southeastern province of Anhui arrived in the mid-nineteenth century. This fourth influence was the famous *pihuang* system, a combination of two melodies, which spread from one end of China to the other to become characteristic of two geographically distant styles, Peking and Cantonese opera.

The last operatic style in the mix that was to become Sichuan opera was *kunqu.* This aristocratic, scholarly, and highly poetic classical drama was brought into Sichuan by its governor in the late nineteenth century. It did not have much popular appeal and *kunqu* actors were forced before long to join fiddle music companies. That movement brought the disparate styles together to produce what is now called Sichuan opera.

Sichuan opera has a strong element of the fantastic, geared to an audience that appreciates stories of ghosts, animal spirits, and demons. It is an opera of myth and legend. The Sichuan opera is unique, for example, in having a clearly delineated role for female ghosts and fox fairies. A special stage technique called 'face changing' expresses contact with the supernatural. As the opera progresses, one man's face grows gradually black with dread in the presence of a ghost, or a spirit goes through a series of terrifying transformations, as can be seen in Chapter 12. The metamorphoses can be handled in a number of ways. A common method calls for the actor to wear several layers of silk gauze, with a different face painted on each one. The actor's face transforms before the audience as he or she deftly removes layers one by one throughout the opera. Acrobatic skills are also a common feature in the Sichuan opera. Ghosts tumble, and terrified mortals try to escape. The awe that these skills win from the audience heightens the sense of magic that pervades the entire form.

Yue Opera
越劇

If Peking opera is the prime theatrical style in Chinese opera, Yue opera is the second. It has the second widest audience of China's regional theatres and represents a relatively new operatic style, having appeared and developed in the twentieth century. Yue opera arises out of the local storytelling and rice-planting songs of Sheng county, in Zhejiang province in southeastern China. In 1906, six village storytellers dressed up and went on stage to perform. They used only a small drum and hand clappers to beat out the rhythm. Hand clappers are different from the clapper or wood block used in clapper opera; two pieces of wood joined by a rope are slung over the hand, like castanets. The wood strips strike each other as the hand flicks

Zhejiang province

the clapper to mark the main beats of the music. The hand clapper produces a sharp 'di' sound, while the small drum produces a 'du' sound. Thus these early twentieth-century performance companies came to be called *didu* troupes.

At first the performers were amateurs who put on shows during village festivals, but *didu* troupes began to gain popularity, and professional companies appeared in the city of Hangzhou, one of China's most important cultural centres. As it spread across the province, *didu* moved away from simple stories of village life to a larger repertoire. Rubbing shoulders with other opera styles engendered a significant development: full orchestration. By 1916, the new opera style was on Shanghai stages, absorbing stories and performance technique from the dominant Great Shaoxing opera, imported from Zhejiang province earlier. It was no longer known as *didu* but as Civil Shaoxing opera, to distinguish it from its competitor. It used costumes and make-up, and singing was supported by the fiddle and flute.

Chinese opera companies were customarily segregated into all-male and all-female troupes. The first all-female troupes for Civil Shaoxing opera were formed in the early 1920s. They were so successful that by the mid-1930s the female companies had completely replaced the male ones, making this new opera style synonymous with female performers. It now began to be called Yue opera because in ancient times the Zhejiang region was known as the state of Yue. Yue opera took another great step in its development in 1943, when the famous actress Yuan Xuefen experimented with a series of modifications to the form. The results were the introduction of opera directors, new costume designs, colourful make-up, extensive scenery, and lighting. Much of the impetus for reform came from Western-style stage drama and popular film.

Yue opera programs not only rework classical stories but also present new pieces with contemporary themes. The singing and acting style is expressive and emotional, drawing on modern dramatic techniques. Men have made their way back onto the Yue opera stage, but its reputation still rests on the performance and innovations of women.

Shaoxing Opera
紹劇

Shaoxing, in present-day Zhejiang, was the capital of the ancient state of Yue. The city has been a commercial and cultural centre throughout history, and thus has had an important role in the development of Chinese drama.

Various musical styles from different regions arrived in Shaoxing at the end of the Ming and beginning of the Qing dynasties. One of those styles was from Yiyang, a city in the southern province of Jiangxi. *Yiyang* music was predominantly percussive and immensely popular. The other style was *luantan*, a clapper opera technique accompanied primarily by strings. One of the most influential singing styles in the sixteenth century came out of the nearby town of Yuyao. In the Ming dynasty, a seated storyteller used the *yuyao* singing style with a percussion accompaniment to present a story, taking different roles as it unfolded. Shaoxing theatre companies that adopted this storytelling technique for opera became known as 'high melodic' troupes. Performers in Shaoxing blended these musical systems into the local singing style, but before long the clapper style dominated. This regional opera was even called Shaoxing Clapper opera for a time.

Shaoxing opera is accompanied primarily by the wooden fiddle and sometimes supported by the small lute. The music is forceful and the singing style is exaggerated. Actors are not strictly limited by the music, but can embellish their arias according to the mood of the scene. Acting technique is characterized by large, bold gestures and stylized martial arts based on a local fighting method. Actors use a full voice range from the natural to the falsetto. This larger-than-life performance style and energetic music is particularly suitable for the Shaoxing opera repertoire of historical pieces, many of which give the actors opportunity to display anger and portray struggle.

This operatic form established itself in Shanghai early in the twentieth century to become a leading theatrical style there. Its heyday was short-lived, however, as the Shaoxing opera began to lose its audience to both the fresh Yue opera and the popular Peking opera.

Anhui (Hui) Opera
徽劇

Regional opera from the southeastern province of Anhui has had an enormous effect on opera throughout China. At least forty different opera styles from north to south have incorporated Anhui operatic musical form, which first grew out of two musical styles that made their way into the province in the sixteenth century. The first was the powerful and percussive *yiyang* style from the southeast. The second was the eastern *yuyao* style. The *yuyao* style was, like its counterpart, also percussive. It was also characterized by 'rolling passages': parenthetical sections of song or speech. They could appear at any time and were usually delivered very quickly, with many syllables to a single note. Rolling passages served to clarify a particular aria or the plot line itself by adding detail and exposition. *Yiyang* and *yuyao* combined to produce a local Anhui style, which relied on a chorus and did not require strings or winds.

The style was modified near the end of the Ming dynasty with the arrival of the classical opera from the south, *kunqu*. The chorus was discarded but flute accompaniment was adopted. This new, more refined opera called for singing and dance. It went through another transformation at the beginning of China's last dynasty, the Qing, when clapper opera was performed in Anhui. A solemn, sedate melodic pattern

Anhui province

called *erhuang* and a lively, upbeat form called *xipi,* both derived from clapper opera, were merged into the *pihuang* style, originally accompanied by a flute, then by an oboe-like instrument called the *suona,* and finally by a lead violin.

Anhui was a powerful centre of commerce and culture; its merchants and officials travelled throughout China on business. An audience for the new music thus grew up in many places, as travelling companies took *pihuang* drama, or Anhui opera – in China known as Hui opera – to many great cities. Its arrival in Beijing in 1790 is credited as the birth or impetus for the growth of a new style, the Peking opera. The Anhui opera's *pihuang* music, bold performance technique, and use of special skills from acrobatics to knife throwing made a strong impression at the capital. Anhui's vital role in forming the Peking opera, however, was also the beginning of its demise, as audiences and actors shifted to the new style. Anhui opera did, however, maintain a presence in Beijing from 1790 right into the twentieth century, and in recent years has made a comeback. With such varied roots, it has a large and rich repertoire.

Huangmei Opera
黃梅戲

Despite the influence of Anhui opera in the past, it is Huangmei opera that has become the province's chief regional drama. It grew up in Huaining county along the banks of the Yangtze river, which runs through Anhui. Huangmei tea-picking music – which takes its name from a district in Hubei and was sung in both provinces – was a popular folk performance art that had spread to many different areas. Music that adopted the Huaining dialect became known as the Huai singing style and was the forerunner of Huangmei opera. This song and dance entertainment gradually evolved in the nineteenth century into a little theatre style performed by peasants and artisans at festivals. It absorbed some of the music and performance technique of Anhui opera and began to present complete stories in a clapper music format. The new style still preserved the natural quality of the peasant folk dance, and performers still sang while they danced. The music was entirely percussive and usually played by three musicians. Seven performers acted out the story with props and costumes taken entirely from daily life. The stage was either simply an empty space or ox carts pushed together to make an impromptu platform.

Professional troupes began to appear in the twentieth century and moved from the villages to the cities. By 1931, the city of Anqing had two permanent companies. The new form underwent a great change when a company travelled out of Anhui to Shanghai. The Peking opera and other regional styles performed in Shanghai made a deep impression on the Huangmei opera. Several new pieces entered its repertoire, and Huangmei music underwent revision. Clapper music was discarded, and the Peking fiddle – a slightly smaller and higher-pitched version of the Chinese second fiddle – was introduced into the orchestration. Since then, Huangmei opera has incorporated folk songs and developed the orchestration so that it is now one of the most melodic of all the regional operas. The music is gentle and sung in a natural voice. Musical instruments from various regions of China as well as from the West are now used. That performers sing while dancing is a direct link back to the tea-picking performance art from which the opera arose. Huangmei opera uses the official speech of Anqing as its stage language. Dialogue is in the vernacular and easily understood by the audience. The performance technique is expressive, emotional, and soft. Huangmei opera has become the most popular regional opera form in Anhui and has spread to several other provinces. Over fifty cities in eight provinces have professional Huangmei companies in addition to many amateur troupes. Several popular films have been made using the Huangmei style.

Jiangxi (Gan) Opera
贛劇

In China, opera from Jiangxi province is known as Gan opera after the Gan river, which runs almost the entire length of the province from south to north. The southeastern province of Jiangxi is strategically located for the development of regional opera. It borders on the provinces of Anhui, famous for its *pihuang* music, and Zhejiang, a performance centre for *kunqu*. These musical styles played a role in the mix that was to become Jiangxi opera, but the most important element was high music. The high music of the Jiangxi opera was a blend of the *yiyang* style from northern Jiangxi and the *qingyang* singing style from Anhui. They blended well because both employed percussion instruments rather than strings and winds, parenthetical rolling passages, and a chorus to back up a main singer who performed in colloquial speech. There were differences, however. Whereas the *yiyang* style was strong and bright, *qingyang* singing was gentle. *Yiyang* was used for historical dramas such as tales from *The Romance of the Three Kingdoms*, and *qingyang* was used more often for the poetic Ming dramas called *chuanqi*. Together the two formed a more complete system with a broader range.

That system, high music, has had a strong impact on the development of Chinese opera. Thirty-seven opera styles in eleven provinces have incorporated it. Jiangxi opera grew from this important root, adopting local storytelling music early in its development. At the beginning of the Qing dynasty, elements of *kunqu* made their way in, as did elements of clapper opera at the beginning of the twentieth century.

The result is an opera rich in orchestration, particularly for transitional passages between sections or scenes. The Chinese oboe, flute, and strings are all used. The many different traditions that have contributed to the Jiangxi opera have provided it with a gamut of dramas from historical epics to romances. Actors use a formalized performance technique, but it is not as strict as the one used in Peking opera.

Jiangxi province

Actors entering the stage will present themselves to stage right, centre stage, and stage left before performing, for example, a technique that grew out of the practice of addressing an audience surrounding a raised wooden or bamboo stage during an outdoor performance. At the same time, the form is simple and direct, using sharply defined, realistic mime movements and referring to elements of country life such as fishing and daily tasks.

Cantonese (Yue) Opera
粵劇

Cantonese opera – named after the city of Canton, now Guangzhou – is the most popular theatrical form in the southern province of Guangdong and has a presence in Chinese communities throughout the world. (In China, it is known as Yue opera, though this is not to be confused with the Yue opera style from Zhejiang province.) It has, in addition, a long history. Troupes in Guangdong have used local singing styles to perform plays in Cantonese since the sixteenth century. These actors developed Cantonese opera by incorporating *kunqu*, southern *yiyang* melodies, and clapper opera.

Its rapid development was seriously set back when the Qing court forbade all performance of Cantonese opera in 1854. A talented Cantonese opera star had led actors in a revolt against the dynasty, taken cities, and established his own kingdom. After the rebellion failed, the central government attacked the local opera as the seat of sedition and banned it for fourteen years. Some companies tried to pass themselves off as Peking opera troupes, but a great many actors simply joined other regional drama companies. When the ban was lifted, however, these actors brought a rich variety of experience in other operas back to their beloved local Cantonese opera.

One of the results of this mix was that the *pihuang* singing style of Anhui opera began to dominate the music. Cantonese *pihuang* uses the same melodic structure as Peking opera but the orchestration remains typically southern. The flute, Chinese oboe, and strings provide a gentle, melodic accompaniment. Cantonese orchestration has been the object of no end of experimentation, involving, in this century, violins, saxophones, and electric guitars.

Cantonese opera underwent various changes in the 1920s. The high falsetto singing derived from clapper opera was replaced by the natural voice; an official stage Cantonese was replaced by colloquial speech; operas on contemporary themes were added to the repertoire; and scenery and special effects were adopted. The young man's role and the clown's role gained prominence in the 1930s through the work of two talented actors. Xue Juexian drew on Peking opera performance style in his portrayal of the young man. Ma Shizeng made use of the more natural performance style of modern, spoken drama in his portrayal of the clown.

Guangdong province

Cantonese opera has kept its popularity. While maintaining a body of traditional pieces, it performs fresh operas and continues to experiment with staging and performance technique.

Chaozhou Opera
潮劇

Chaozhou is a region in the northeastern corner of Guangdong province. It boasts a regional drama, Chaozhou opera, with one of the longest histories of China's local theatres. A Chaozhou opera on the stage in the mid-sixteenth century quickly became popular throughout Guangdong and spread into the neighbouring province of Fujian. It was actually a regionalized form of the southern drama, which appeared in southern China during the Song and Yuan dynasties.

The stability of the Ming dynasty and improved transportation routes brought about the rapid spread of four great musical styles associated with this period: *yiyang, yuyao, haiyan,* and *kunqu,* all of which arose in southeastern China. (*Yuyao* and *haiyan* have not survived.) These four entered the Chaozhou region and made their impression on regional opera there. Later musical developments like clapper and *pihuang* also affected Chaozhou opera. The opera that has emerged uses song suites and a variable rhythmic structure. The music is melodious, precise, and intricate. Chaozhou opera orchestration relies primarily on strings and the Chinese oboe, but also uses the flute and percussion instruments. One of its main characteristics is the use of a chorus to sing with a main character throughout an aria or to round off an aria after the character has finished.

Comedy is a strong feature of Chaozhou opera. It has ten different kinds of clowns, who play officials, generals, peasants, and scholars. They often imitate animals, perform in a manner reminiscent of puppetry, and use fans as props to distinguish their role types.

Traditional plays number over 1,200. There are two main types of Chaozhou programs. The first comes from the southern drama and *chuanqi* tradition and includes classics such as *The Lute.* The second is a collection of local legends that includes ghost stories. These plays in particular have a strong regional flavour. The clothes, scenery, and props, including lanterns and cut-paper decorations, are all in the Chaozhou folk art style.

Chapter 3   Conventions

REGIONAL OPERATIC FORMS differ chiefly in dialect and music, but traditional stage conventions of Chinese opera are consistent. They offer a stage language that represents rather than re-creates stories. Gestures, costumes, and props are used as symbols, not as elements of literal portrayal. Many regional opera styles are now incorporating realistic scenery, lighting, and special effects alongside traditional Chinese stage technique.

The Stage

Chinese drama has been performed in temple courtyards and palaces, in village squares and mansions, on boats and in teahouses. The traditional Chinese stage protrudes and thus is open to the audience on three sides. Two pillars, one on each side of the front corners, support a roof. Although the pillars block the view, the audience has more mobility than in a Western-style theatre. Some people stand at the front and others move around as needed. A low railing runs around the sides exposed to the audience. Two doors, one on either side of the back, are used for entrances and exits. Entrances are made through the door on stage right; exits are made through the door on stage left. The exception to the rule is for characters who are re-entering a scene, having, for example, gone into a tent and come back out of it. In these cases the stage-left door is used. The musicians take their place at the rear corner of stage right, in full view of the audience. From this vantage point the musicians can watch the proceedings and interact with the performers in a lively, integrated way. The performance takes place mostly at the front of the stage, but scenes involving battles and acrobatics make full use of the stage space. That space is usually bare except for an embroidered curtain at the rear and a carpet.

Many temple courtyards boasted permanent stages. Troupes were invited to perform plays there on the deity's birthday and other festive days. The performance faced the deity to whom it was directed. A modern adaptation is the positioning of a television set, tuned to a local station for the evening, suspended from a temple ceiling and facing the god. Temporary stages made from bamboo poles, mats, and wooden planks were erected in market squares or at temples without permanent stages. These are still erected for travelling companies today. Teahouses that incorporated permanent stages were immensely popular in the nineteenth century.

3.1
A Hebei Clapper opera orchestra, seated stage left and seen from the wings.

3.2
Qing dynasty theatre in Suzhou. The performance took place on the upper level. The audience watched from the surrounding galleries and open courtyard.

3.3
A village theatre performance demonstrating a blend of classical and modern practices. The musicians sit in the traditional stage right position, in view of the audience. The performance is on a modern Western-style stage and uses a realistic set.

Patrons sat on stools or benches drinking tea, eating snacks, chatting through performances, and shouting 'hao,' or bravo, at particularly well-executed moments. Today, Chinese operas are usually performed on Western-style proscenium stages equipped with modern lighting. All of the photographs in this book are of this type. Operas performed in the traditional manner treat the proscenium stage in a similar way to the traditional thrust stage. Actors make their entrances from stage right and exit stage left. Lighting is full and even. The musicians are still on the stage, but have moved across to stage left and are tucked just inside the curtain. Experimental drama, on the other hand, makes full use of lighting and sound effects, scenery, and whatever device modern theatre has to offer. Several regional opera styles, like the Cantonese opera and the Yue opera, have adopted much Western stage technique into their presentations.

Props

Gesture and mime accomplish a great deal on the traditional Chinese stage. Actors execute familiar movements that indicate unbolting and opening a door, for example, and stepping over a threshold. Scenery is not needed to establish place. A character announces the start of a journey and simply walks in a circle on the stage. Upon completing the circle, the character announces that he or she has arrived at the destination. Thus props and scenery are reduced to a minimum. Even these are often only suggestive, requiring some mime to complete the representation. The horse whip representing a horse has already been mentioned. The whip comes to a life as a horse only through the precise mime of mounting, riding, and dismounting. The paddle is a similar prop. An actor manipulates a paddle, coordinating it with swaying and floating movements of passengers to present the delightful impression of a boat.

Whereas the paddle and whip are drawn from daily life, flags are used in a more abstract sense and have a wide range of signification. A black flag indicates a great wind. A flag with a wave design indicates a flood. Two flags with a picture of a wheel on each make a chariot when held by a servant on either side of the passenger. Small pennants attached to the back of a general stand for the battalions under his command.

Props like cups or chairs are brought on stage and removed by plainly dressed stagehands during the course of a performance, in front of the audience. The stagehands also rearrange the furniture for different scenes. The customary arrangement of a sitting room is a narrow table with a chair on each side, positioned slightly to the front and on a diagonal. Stagehands simply add additional chairs to make the scene the imperial court. A chair behind the table makes the throne. Should they put the chair on top of the table, they make a mountain or a high platform. If the table and chairs are removed, the actors can use the stage as a roadway or a battlefield.

3.4
Backstage at the Cantonese opera. Tasselled horse whips lie on the table in the foreground underneath coronets worn by officials.

An actor carrying a lantern indicates to the audience that it is night without any change in the lighting.

Props and furniture make the stage space fluid. In the hands of the actors they are tools that readily transform the stage from one place into another without ambiguity.

Musical Instruments

Chapter 2 discussed a number of musical styles. The orchestra that plays these styles is divided into two parts according to the type of instrument. The *wen*, or civil section, is composed of string and wind instruments. The *wu*, or military section, is composed of percussion instruments. The civil section accompanies the singing of scholars, beauties, and so on, whereas the military section accompanies battle scenes, hand-to-hand combat, and the like. The main instruments of traditional Chinese drama are described below. As pointed out earlier, variations and experiments have widened the orchestral range for both particular opera types and particular operas.

Stringed Instruments

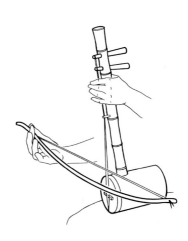

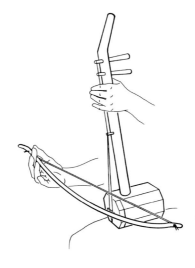

Fiddles *(huqin)*

The first fiddle *(jinghu)*

The Chinese fiddle has two strings and is the main stringed instrument in the *pihuang* musical style. A bow made of horsehair is passed between the strings of the instrument. The bow thus comes in contact with the inside of one string and the outside of the other, alternating from one to the other as it is bowed back and forth. The fiddle has a shrill, piercing sound that is amplified through a snakeskin-covered sound box open at the back. It is held upright on the musician's knee.

The second fiddle *(erhu)*

The second fiddle is a little larger than the first fiddle and has a large sound box. The sound is thus deeper and softer. The *erhu* is held in the same manner as the *jinghu*.

The wood-faced fiddle *(banhu)*

The wood-faced fiddle is used in clapper opera. While the snakeskin-covered sound box of the first fiddle used in Peking opera produces a piercing sound, the wooden cover of the sound box of this instrument produces a penetrating but less shrill tone. The instrument is held upright on the player's knee.

The three-stringed banjo *(sanxian)*

Like the Western banjo, the three-stringed banjo is plucked rather than bowed. It produces a shallow, twangy sound. Three gut strings run across a snakeskin sound box, up a long neck without frets, to tuning pegs.

The moon guitar *(yueqin)*

The moon guitar gets its name from a large, round wooden sound box. Like the banjo, it is plucked with a plectrum rather than bowed and is held vertically on the performer's knee. Unlike the banjo, however, the moon guitar has four strings and frets on a short neck.

The lute *(pipa)*

The lute is a four-stringed, fretted instrument with a teardrop-shaped sound box. It is strummed and plucked like the moon guitar. Possessing an extraordinary range of sound, it can accompany plaintive songs and produce the violence of a heated battle. The lute is held upright on the knee.

Wind Instruments

The vertical flute *(xiao)*

The vertical flute is a five-holed instrument held in much the same way as a clarinet. It produces a deep, airy sound.

The transverse flute *(dizi)*

The vertical flute is held and played much like the Western flute but has eight or ten holes rather than keys. The transverse flute produces a bright and lively sound in a higher register than the *xiao*.

The reed organ *(sheng)*

The *sheng* is a collection of bamboo tubes in varying lengths, fixed in a base. A mouthpiece at the side carries air into the tubes for a sound similar to a harmonica. The musician, who is usually standing, holds the base of the instrument level to his or her mouth and blows into the mouthpiece.

The Chinese oboe *(suona)*

The *suona* is a double-reeded wind instrument with a large, flared opening like a horn. It has the powerful volume of a trumpet but the sound quality of bagpipes. The *suona* is often used to imitate high-spirited horses, to announce important arrivals or events, and to signal transitions between scenes. The player holds it as one would a trumpet.

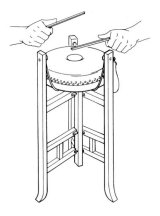

The small, or single, drum *(danpigu)*

The leader of the orchestra plays the small drum. The drummer is attentive to the action on the stage and provides the other musicians with their cues. These are given in a number of ways. The position of the two bamboo drumsticks on the drum or how they are held are preparatory gestures to musical forms. The drum's leather skin is tightly drawn over a wooden frame about twenty-five centimetres across. The drummer sits behind the three-legged stand that holds the drum. The instrument produces a high, crisp, wooden sound that carries far.

The large drum *(dagu)*

Military or festive scenes will sometimes use the large drum. This drum stands upright and gives a deep, resonant sound similar to but not quite as reverberant as a tympani. The musician is seated while playing the instrument.

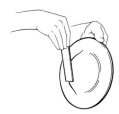

The small gong *(xiaolo)*

This smaller version of the gong has a distinctively high-pitched, almost tinny sound. The small gong is often played by itself, particularly when a female lead character enters. One hand grasps a lip at the back of the gong, and the other uses a flat stick to strike the centre.

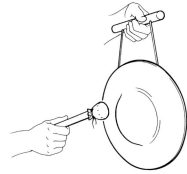

The large gong *(dalo)*

The large gong is much the same sort of gong as that used in the Western orchestra, although somewhat smaller. The musician holds the brass gong with one hand from a handle at the top and strikes it with the other hand. It produces deep reverberations and is often used at particularly exciting moments.

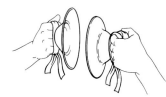

The cymbals *(bo)*

The cymbals are two hollow, bell-shaped metal instruments that usually have a long, decorative scarf-like piece of cloth attached to the back of each. The musician holds one in each hand by grasping the cloth and clangs them together for a sharp, strong sound.

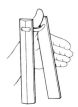

Hand clappers *(ban)*

The orchestra leader also plays hand clappers. This castanet-like instrument is made up of three pieces of wood, each about thirty centimetres long. Two of the pieces are fitted flush against one another to form one side of the instrument. The side made of a single piece of wood fits in the palm. The two sides are loosely joined by a loop of cord at one end and supported by the musicians' left thumb. The paired pieces then hang down in the palm, on either side of the thumb. The leader swings one piece across the other for a sharp sound that keeps rhythm, signals musical forms, and punctuates the performance.

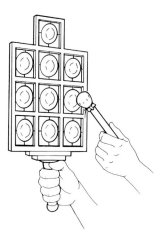

Cloud gongs *(yunlo)*

Ten little gongs, each half the size of the small gong, hang in a wooden frame. Each gong is tuned to a different note of the scale. The musician can thus play clear, ringing melodic lines, holding the frame by a handle at the base.

Role Types

Actors in traditional Chinese theatre each train for a specific role type. Although a play has its own personae, they all fit into predetermined categories. Each category has its own singing and speaking style, movements, and appropriate costume. The subdivisions within the categories vary from one regional form to another, but generally speaking there are four main role types: *dan, sheng, jing,* and *chou*. Those discussed below are found in the Peking opera, but as the photographs show, variations on them occur in China's many regional operatic forms.

Female Role *(Dan)*

The singing and acting style for the female role was developed and fine-tuned by men. There are several subcategories, of which only a few will be discussed here.

The *qingyi*, the young maiden, is one of the most important female role types. Her graceful steps, delicate movements, and falsetto voice present her as a paragon of Confucian virtues. She uses long sleeves, called water sleeves, that drape nearly to her feet for a wide variety of expression.

Another subcategory of the *dan* is the *guimendan*, the 'private-quarters woman.' She is from a wealthy family and is set apart from the world in the family mansion.

The *huadan* is less of a paragon but more lively. She is often the feisty servant girl, and whereas the *qingyi* role emphasizes singing, the *huadan* role emphasizes high spirits.

Actors performing these roles wear elaborate coiffures and full white make-up accented with rouge that goes across the cheeks and sweeps up to elongated eyes. The eyes themselves are circled with rouge.

3.5
The young maiden (qingyi) exudes refinement with her delicate movements, mincing steps, and exaggerated falsetto singing. Peking opera

3.6
The refined 'private-quarters woman' role (guimendan) wears rich clothing and an elaborate coiffure. Her gestures are graceful and delicate. Yue opera

3.7
The lively maiden (huadan) is the sprightly counterpart to the qingyi. Her role emphasizes speech and gesture more than singing. Peking opera

Another major female role is the *laodan*, or old woman. She appears with little or no make-up, a head band, and a walking staff. The role encompasses a broad variety of types: helpless victim, powerful matriarch, adviser to the *qingyi*, or any number of others.

As will be discussed in Chapter 6, women also have military roles to play on the Chinese opera stage. The *wudan*, or warrior woman, demonstrates her prowess with weapons, chiefly swords and spears. Although her make-up is the same as the *qingyi*, she does not have water sleeves. She wears more functional costumes to enable her to perform her military skills.

A variant of the *wudan* is the *daomadan*, literally 'weapon and horse woman.' Like the *wudan* she is a spirited fighter, but her actions are not as violent or as quick. Her role contains more singing and beautiful movement akin to dance.

3.8
The old woman (laodan), on the right in this photograph, has minimal make-up and wears a cloth band around her head. Jiangxi opera

3.9
The warrior woman (wudan) wears a close-fitting costume and is adept at rapidly handling weapons in battle. Peking opera

3.10
The elegant 'weapon and horse woman' (daomadan) is dressed in full armour and ready for battle. Jiangxi opera

Male Role *(Sheng)*

The *xiaosheng*, the young man, is the opera counterpart for the *qingyi*. He is usually a young scholar or prince who, like the young maiden, uses water sleeves for refined expression, and even breaks into falsetto in both song and speech. Even his make-up bears some resemblance to that used on the female lead, generally white with rouge highlights.

The *laosheng*, the old man's role, like the old woman's role, uses little make-up. He has a long, white beard and often wears a plain costume. This role is particularly valued for its singing and for the virtues of loyalty and uprightness that it presents on the stage.

The *wusheng*, or warrior, is an acrobatic role. He is the fierce fighter, capable with a wide range of weaponry. He can appear in a range of costume from the splendid embroidered armour of a general to the simple clothes of a fugitive. If he wears armour and supports pennants on his back, he belongs to the armoured warrior group *(changkaowusheng)*. This character meets his opponents primarily with long spears. If he appears without armour, he belongs to the close-combat warrior group *(duandawusheng)*, which fights with more acrobatics and hand-to-hand technique than the armoured warrior group.

3.11
The young man (xiaosheng) *has long water sleeves, a white and rouge face, and a falsetto vocal style. In this photograph the role is played by a woman. Yue opera*

3.12
The old man (laosheng) *is characterized by his long beard, minimal make-up, and expressive singing style. Cantonese opera*

3.13
The close-combat warrior (duandawusheng) *is an acrobatic fighter. Kunqu opera*

The painted-face characters are a powerfully arresting component of Chinese theatre. Brilliant, bold colours and designs painted directly on the face communicate the identity and personality of this male character. A predominantly white face, for example, indicates treachery and craftiness; a black one indicates impartiality and uprightness, as for the honest judge of *Judge Bao's Apology* (see Chapter 7). A large band of cloth is pulled around the forehead of the actor to enlarge the face before make-up is applied. All *jing* characters have painted faces, ranging from a predominant colour to complicated designs. Not all characters with painted face designs belong to this role type, however. The *jing* role also involves a powerful, nasal singing style.

Some characters with painted faces traditionally sing in a different manner and consequently belong to other role types. Guan Yu, for example, one of the three sworn brothers in the *Three Kingdoms* stories found in Chapter 6, appears in the photographs to be *jing* but is actually a *hongsheng,* a special category of

3.14
The armoured warrior (changkaowusheng) *wears armour complete with pennants and wields a spear. Peking opera*

3.15
The painted face (jing) *has bold make-up, padded shoulders, and a forceful singing style. Peking opera*

Clown (Chou)

laosheng, the old man's role. Generals, villains, and supernatural beings are often, though not always, painted-face roles.

Everything about the painted-face role type contributes to a sense of being larger than life. Apart from singing in a forceful voice, the *jing* wears imposing costumes with high, heavy shoes, and large, padded shoulders. He thus takes possession of the stage, drawing all attention to himself as soon as he steps upon it.

The clown can be a source of comic relief or a villain. This character speaks in normal range and in the most colloquial speech of all the characters in a play. The clown can improvise and even bring in references to modern or local events. The characteristic make-up is a small mask-like application of white around the eyes and nose. Several hundred years ago, the clown and painted-face roles were one, but they have since diverged. Whereas the painted face is larger than life and imposing, the clown is down to earth, and speaks in the vernacular.

There are both male and female clowns; generally they are commoners, but there are a few upper-class clowns. Clown make-up is also used for the mean-spirited – and distinctly unfunny – villain.

The female clown, however, does not use the white patch for her make-up. She has a reddened face with blackened eyebrows and often a spot of headache medicine rubbed on her forehead.

3.16
The male clown (chou) has a distinctive white patch of make-up around the nose and speaks in the vernacular. Sichuan opera

3.17
Unlike the male clown, the female clown does not have the white patch of make-up around the nose. Instead, simple make-up exaggerates her features. Yue opera

Chapter 4   Heavenly Beings

HEAVEN IS BOTH immediate and familiar in China. Divination, honouring one's ancestors, and propitiating the gods are all practical acts underscoring that our world and the world of the spirits are woven together. The two worlds are so intertwined that they work in much the same way. Heaven, like earth, manages its affairs through an appointed bureaucracy. The Jade Emperor in heaven, like his counterpart in the Middle Kingdom (China), rules through officials and departments staffed by heavenly civil servants. The Chinese, having experienced centuries of bureaucratic administration, know the strengths and shortcomings of such a system both on earth and in heaven.

Heaven is a very tolerant place. It has room for figures from both Taoism and Buddhism. The great Taoist philosopher Laozi, the Buddhist dispenser of compassion Guanyin, or the Goddess of Mercy, and China's Eight Immortals can be found attending the same banquets there. No one raises an eyebrow. These heavenly beings are certainly more exalted than we are, but they are fallible and therefore approachable.

Instead of solemn reverence, Chinese drama treats heaven and heavenly beings sometimes with mirth and even sometimes with disapproval. In *Monkey Business in Heaven* an upstart monkey king crashes heaven with delightful irreverence. He makes fools of the heavenly bureaucrats, who are helpless to stop him without intervention from Buddha. Later Monkey accompanies a holy monk on a journey to India. The monk constantly gets them into trouble with his bumbling naïveté, and it is Monkey, with his energy and good, solid sense, that gets them out of it time after time. In other plays the Eight Immortals get drunk, behave badly, and in the end look sheepish when bested by others.

Heaven and earth come closest together in forbidden love stories. A heavenly being falls in love with a mortal in violation of all the rules. Heaven, of course, sends out its emissaries to stop these unnatural unions. Yet when these stories play themselves out on the stage, the sympathy is clearly against heaven and its representatives for trying to interfere. The audience pulls for the lovers, not for the Buddhist priests or heavenly warriors.

Thus human values are the important ones; humans can be warmer, cleverer, and more generous than heavenly beings. Heaven has its power, but it has its failings too, and self-importance is to be ridiculed anywhere.

4.1
The heavenly beings, in The Legend of the White Snake. *Sichuan opera.*

The Hibiscus Fairy
芙蓉花仙
Sichuan Opera

The Hibiscus Fairy is a traditional Sichuan drama that was radically reworked by a county opera troupe in 1981. The new play is experimental opera that combines ballet, magic, and folk music with traditional acrobatics and martial arts. Originally about a fairy consorting with other heavenly beings, in the new version *The Hibiscus Fairy* has become a love story about overcoming the gulf between the human and the divine. It declares the right of lovers to claim their own happiness and make their own destiny.

Once there was a beautiful garden all in bloom. The gardener, Chen Qiulin, carrying his hoe over his shoulder, arrived to tend the flowers. He watered them one by one until he came across the hibiscus. He sighed for her. How wonderful it would be if this delicate flower were human. Why, she could come to his room in the evening to talk of poetry and beautiful things!

That night, as Chen Qiulin sat alone in his room the wind carried in an exquisite perfume of hibiscus. The moment he recognized it, he saw before him a beautiful woman. The flower spirit had come to him in human form. Their time together was brief and as suddenly as she had appeared, so she suddenly left him. But she was not really gone. The Hibiscus Fairy watched Chen Qiulin secretly as he wrote a poem to her. When the rumblings of a thunderstorm threatened the garden, the gardener hurried out to protect the hibiscus. The fairy, deeply moved, was on the point of appearing to him again when the spirits of wind and rain materialized, seized her, and took her away.

The Goddess of the Hundred Flowers had sent these spirits to take the Hibiscus Fairy prisoner. How dare the fairy fall in love with a mortal! That was breaking all the rules. But the Hibiscus Fairy was unrepentant. What was wrong with loving a mortal? Did she not in fact grow in the world of humankind? The goddess was enraged and determined to kill the Hibiscus Fairy, but the other flower spirits interceded for her and won a lighter sentence, exile to Cold Spring Mountain near the southern city of Yangzhou. The Banana Spirit was appointed to guard her carefully. That was a fateful decision.

The Hibiscus Fairy endured her exile for seven months, all the time thinking of Chen Qiulin. He, in the meantime, had made plans to go to Yangzhou to study under his uncle. His road took him over Cold Spring Mountain. Walking along, he suddenly smelled a familiar fragrance. He looked up and there saw a hibiscus plant. It seemed sickly. The leaves were about to drop off and the earth around it was very dry. So Chen Qiulin brought water to it and loosened the soil. Wishing the plant well, the gardener continued on his way. The Hibiscus Fairy materialized and made to follow him but found her way barred by the Banana Spirit. She begged him to let her go. The Banana Spirit, however, had other ideas. He told her that humans were meant for humans and spirits were meant for spirits. He would be a much more suitable match for her! The Hibiscus Fairy refused him, and the Banana Spirit tried to take her by force. She struggled furiously, managed to repulse him, and got away.

4.2 *(facing page)*
The Hibiscus Fairy takes human form to dance
with the flower spirits in the garden. Sichuan opera

4.3
The Hibiscus Fairy dances. Sichuan opera

Chen Qiulin arrived at his uncle's house in Yangzhou only to find himself under pressure to marry Uncle Su's daughter. Determined to have his way, Su finally tricked Chen Qiulin into agreeing to the marriage. The next night, the Hibiscus Fairy appeared to Chen Qiulin, insisting that he need not honour such a promise; it would be better if he ran away with her. He agreed to her plan and the two decided to flee the next morning.

The Banana Spirit anticipated that the lovers would try to run off together. They would surely try to cross the river and get as far away from Yangzhou as possible, so he transformed himself into a boatman, a banana leaf into a boat, and a tree spirit into his assistant. The Hibiscus Fairy and Chen Qiulin arrived as expected and took the Banana Spirit's boat into the river. Halfway through the trip, the boatman turned back into the Banana Spirit. Grasping his sword, he turned on the fairy. In the fierce battle, she cried out for all the flower spirits along the shore to come to her aid. They flocked to her at once and forced the banana and tree spirits overboard, where they were finally defeated. Free from her persecutor, the Hibiscus Fairy rejoined Chen Qiulin, and the two ran off into the country to find happiness together.

4.4
The Hibiscus Fairy appears to her beloved Chen Qiulin to tell him that he has been tricked by Uncle Su into marrying another. Sichuan opera

4.5 (facing page)
The Banana Spirit, adorned in green leaves, has designs on the Hibiscus Fairy. Sichuan opera

The Hibiscus Fairy

The Legend of the White Snake
白蛇傳
Sichuan, Chaozhou, and Anhui Opera

The Legend of the White Snake is a much-loved story that has been revised and refined over hundreds of years. Originally a violent and evil demon in the earlier stories, White Snake has evolved into a noble heroine who, like the Hibiscus Fairy, risks everything for her love of a mortal. A monk, Fahai, who was a righteous and holy instrument of heaven in earlier tellings, has ended up as an unwelcome spoiler of domestic happiness. This change reflects a modern attitude in China that upholds the right of these characters to forge their happiness in defiance of the hierarchy of heaven. The story has had a lasting presence and still holds a lively place in literature and the performing arts.

In the White Lotus Pool at Emei Mountain in the province of Sichuan lived a white snake. Some say that the beginning of this story was in the distant past, when a young man saved the life of that snake in an earlier incarnation. Others say that the snake and the man were once heavenly beings who fell in love. Buddha had separated them because the young man was at that time an adept, one of Buddha's great disciples, and romantic affairs were forbidden to him. White Snake was sent to the White Lotus Pool and the disciple was sent into the world of mortals to go through the cycle of reincarnation. But all this happened before this story. Whatever the truth of the matter, the destinies of the snake and the man were bound together.

White Snake spent many long years perfecting herself through Taoist practice. She became very beautiful, generous, and powerful. One day, she determined to go into the world and seek out the man, who had no memory of her in his present incarnation. He was called

Xu Xian and now lived in the glorious city of Hangzhou in southeastern China. Blue Snake, another spiritual being, accompanied White Snake as her servant. The two encountered Xu Xian at China's famed West Lake, where he gallantly lent them an umbrella to protect from the rain what he thought were two beautiful women. Xu Xian fell in love with the mysterious Miss White, and it was not very long before they married. This perfect couple set up house with the blue snake spirit attending to their needs.

Not everyone, however, thought that they were a model couple. The first intrusion on their happiness came from a Taoist priest. He saw by his arts that Xu Xian was married to something inhuman. He denounced Miss White as a monster and challenged her to

drink his potions mixed with powerful incantations. The White Snake was confident that her Taoist powers were stronger. She was right. She drank his medicines with no ill effect.

The next intrusion was more serious. The Buddhist monk Fahai from the Golden Mountain Temple warned Xu Xian that he was living with a snake, not a woman. Xu Xian did not believe this monk, for after all had not the Taoist priest proved false? Fahai challenged Xu Xian to put his accusation to the test and suggested the way. The Dragon Boat Festival was near, when it was the custom to drink a powerful wine mixed with medicine for protection against snake bites. If Miss White could be induced to drink it, she would certainly change back into her true form. Xu Xian accepted the challenge, and on the day urged his wife to drink. She did, but this time her powers were not strong enough: she reverted to her true form. Xu Xian collapsed in fear, and when White Snake returned to human shape she discovered that the shock had killed her husband. She flew to Fairy Mountain to obtain a special herb to revive him. Fighting off the guardian spirits, she took the herb and brought it back to her beloved Xu Xian, who recovered.

The monk Fahai did not give up. He convinced Xu Xian to come to the temple, where he placed him under the umbrella of forgetfulness to subvert the influence of the White Snake. She followed and demanded that the monk release her husband. When he did not, she called up a great army from the sea to assault the temple. Frogs, turtles, and countless other aquatic spirits launched their attack. Fahai countered by invoking warriors from heaven, the most powerful of which was his transformed beggar's bowl. The battle was ferocious, and finally White Snake raised a flood to subdue the temple. Suddenly, she had to retire, weak and in pain because she was carrying a child. The baby in her womb was under the protection of a god, and so White Snake was able to get away to safety.

Meanwhile, Xu Xian escaped and tried to make his way back to his wife by crossing Break Bridge. There he met White Snake, who was regaining her strength. He wanted to speak to her, but Blue Snake upbraided him for his thoughtlessness and ingratitude. Xu Xian was wounded by the justice of her words. He now knew the depth of White Snake's love for him. He truly regretted all that had happened, and the three were reconciled.

Together again, the three went away to escape the persecution of the monk. They

4.6 (facing page)
Blue Snake and White Snake descend in a cloud to the world of human beings. Sichuan opera

4.7
White Snake and Blue Snake, the latter a man in this version, prepare to assault the temple and win back Xu Xian, who is being held there by the monk Fahai. Sichuan opera

The Legend of the White Snake

seemed to have succeeded, and the baby was born. Yet one month after the birth, Fahai tracked them down. He confronted White Snake and used heavenly powers to catch her in his golden beggar's bowl. Finally, he imprisoned her under a tall pagoda as punishment for her unnatural marriage.

Some say that many years later the pagoda collapsed and White Snake regained her freedom. But that is another story.

4.8 (facing page)
The two snake spirits narrowly escape the powerful influence of Fahai's Buddhist staff, a spiritual weapon. Xu Xian is oblivious to everything under the umbrella of forgetfulness. Sichuan opera

4.9
Another of Fahai's spiritual weapons, his begging bowl, takes human form to battle the snake spirit. The monk's bowl will finally overcome White Snake. Sichuan opera

4.10
Blue Snake, a woman in this version, threatens Xu Xian with a sword as he escapes over Break Bridge. White Snake, though feeling betrayed, protects her husband. Anhui opera

4.11 (facing page)
Xu Xian feels deep regret at the suffering his wife has endured for him. Chaozhou opera

The Legend of the White Snake

The Eight Immortals Cross the Sea
八仙過海
Peking Opera

Long ago, some favoured men and women in pursuit of perfection obtained immortality. The Eight Immortals are a band of these blessed beings, and they represent the whole spectrum of human society. Male and female, young and old, rich and poor, able bodied and disabled are found among them. Their chief, Zhong Liquan, carries a feather fan with which he revives the dead. The immortals are regular guests at a great banquet held by the Queen of the Western Heaven to celebrate her birthday. They drink much wine and eat their fill of heavenly peaches. This story happened at the end of one of those great banquets.

The Eight Immortals enjoyed themselves immensely and drank a great deal. They left the party drunk and decided to roam about until the strong drink wore off. Arriving at the shore of the Eastern Sea, the immortals decided it would be pleasant to sail across it. One of their company, Zhang Guolao, cautioned against the plan. Zhang Guolao was a hermit who rode backward on a magic donkey and was versed in divination. He recommended that the group consult the oracles to find out whether or not such a trip was auspicious. The group did not want to wait for that. After all, were they not Taoist adepts? They could handle any trouble that came their way.

What came their way was the Goldfish Fairy. She lived in the Eastern Sea and wanted to know just who these strangers were. The immortal Lü Dongbin, self-satisfied and sure of his Taoist superiority, began to provoke the fairy and make fun of her. The Goldfish Fairy, however, was not one to be teased. She could not endure these drunken, ill-mannered immortals and launched an attack against them. The immortals fought her on the sea as best they could but found all their skills were no match for the fairy. She vanquished them and there was no way out but to eat humble pie, apologize, and go chastened on their way.

4.12
The immortals, having left their heavenly banquet, prepare to cross the sea in a cloud. Peking opera

4.13 (facing page)
The Goldfish Fairy stirs up the waves of the Eastern Sea. Peking opera

The Eight Immortals Cross the Sea

4.14 (facing page)
The Goldfish Fairy displays her fighting skills and
easily deflects a tasselled spear with her foot.
Peking opera

4.15
The immortals are defeated one by one. It is now
Lü Dongbin's turn. Peking opera

Crossing Wits
戲牡丹
Anhui Opera

The Chinese delight in good riddles, which have long been a special part of celebrations and great festivals such as New Year. The Chinese language, with its tones and pictorial writing, permits a wealth of clever puns and jokes. Audiences enjoy *Crossing Wits* not for swiftly executed acrobatics but for its fast-moving, skilful repartee.

The immortal Lü Dongbin once visited the city of Hangzhou with his servant. He strolled about carrying his magic sword and Taoist fly whisk. That no one recognized him just confirmed his own high opinion of his powers. Lü Dongbin stopped in front of a medicine shop and read the sign: 'We have all medicines for all diseases!' He was aghast at the presumption of this little shop and decided to teach the owners a lesson.

Bai Yunlong and his daughter, White Peony, ran their business to do good in the world rather than for profit. Bai Yunlong welcomed the immortal and his servant into his shop, thinking them ordinary customers. What could he do for the gentlemen? Lü Dongbin baited him. Was the shopkeeper sure that he could supply any medicine for any need? Bai Yunlong assured him that he could. What a braggart, thought the immortal. Lü Dongbin then ordered four special medicines: satisfaction tablets, contentment pills, worry cream, and anger powder. Bai Yunlong was taken aback. What kind of medicines were these? He thought fast and pretended that they were temporarily out of stock. Aha! The immortal had caught him out. His sign was just a false boast and should be broken into pieces! Bai Yunlong begged the immortal and his servant not to break his sign but to wait while he checked in the back.

Bai Yunlong talked over the problem with his daughter. White Peony was a clever girl, and she realized at once that the mysterious customer was playing some kind of game. She sent her father away, assuring him that she would handle the situation, and went to face the immortal. White Peony told him that she knew his game: he was making up names to try and show them up. Lü Dongbin was not one to be bested by a shop girl, so he challenged her to a trial of wits. If she could guess his riddles, she could save her sign board. White Peony agreed. Lü Dongbin smiled to himself. It was really too unfair of him – a

common shop girl in a trial of wits with a great Taoist immortal!

The young White Peony waited unconcerned as her customer prepared his questions. First he gave her a number of cryptic medicinal names, believing that she could never guess what the real medicines were. But she guessed every one. Then he posed riddles of heavenly things. She got them all. He tried questions about earthly things. She got all those too. The servant took the immortal aside and advised him to leave before he humiliated himself any more. This person was just too clever for the immortal! Lü Dongbin did not like the sound of that and launched into more riddles, this time referring to the shop girl herself. White Peony had no trouble at all guessing the right answers.

Trying to save the face of his master, the servant tried posing riddles that referred to the immortal. White Peony used each answer to insult this uppity customer who obviously thought so much of himself and so little of her. Finally, exhausted of riddles, Lü Dongbin was speechless. White Peony, however, was not. She advised him not to underestimate people. Don't be so proud, she scolded, because you have just an ordinary mind. You go about feeling so superior but accomplish nothing of importance. Lü Dongbin and the servant slunk away. Imagine being bested by a common shop girl!

4.16
The immortal sits back ready to make a fool of the shop girl. Anhui opera

4.17 (facing page)
The shop girl, White Peony, brings in tea and prepares to make a fool of the immortal. Anhui opera

Stories of the Monkey King

The monkey king, Sun Wukong, is a familiar and favourite character for children and grown-ups. He is full of high energy, mischief, and fun. Any opera with the monkey king in it is sure to dazzle the audience with acrobatics and antics. His stories are found in the famous Ming dynasty novel *Journey to the West,* in which an unlikely band of pilgrims stumbles into amazing adventure after amazing adventure. Chinese audiences know the events well. They delight in the imagination of the stories and in the breathtaking skills needed to bring them to the stage. One of these plays, *Monkey and the White Bone Demon,* warns about evil that arrives in pleasing and disarming disguises. After the Cultural Revolution, it was performed as an attack on Jiang Qing, Chairman Mao's wife. She was now seen as the White Bone Demon, who had come with smiles and greetings from the chairman but was in reality a devourer.

Monkey Business in Heaven
鬧天宮
Peking and Hebei Clapper Opera

Sun Wukong was not just any monkey. He was the king of the monkeys on the Mountain of Flowers and Fruit. He possessed magic skills learned from a Taoist master and wielded a great weapon, a staff won from the Dragon King of the Eastern Sea beneath the water. Having searched the earth and the seas for their secrets, the audacious Sun Wukong turned his attention to heaven. He ascended to paradise, where he pointed out to the heavenly court that his cleverness and great abilities entitled him to both a title and a position in the heavenly bureaucracy. He had come for a job.

The Jade Emperor reluctantly agreed to Monkey's outrageous proposed title, Great Sage Equal to Heaven, and gave him a job in the stables. Monkey wanted a more prestigious appointment than that and finally found himself tending heaven's own peach orchard. These particular peaches were great treasures because once ripe, and they only ripened every 3,000 years, they conferred immortality on whoever ate them.

The Queen of the Western Heaven prepared for her great peach banquet; it was going to be a wonderful affair. She invited the Eight Immortals, the Goddess of Mercy, and other assorted heavenly celebrities. The queen did not, however, invite Monkey. Sun Wukong decided that the only thing to do was to invite himself. He sneaked into the banquet before the feast began and glutted himself on peaches. The mischie-vous monkey king then flew to the alchemy studio of the founder of Taoism, Laozi, and swallowed up all his magic pills. With that, he quit heaven and returned to his monkey friends on the Mountain of Flowers and Fruit.

Heaven sent its forces out after the audacious Monkey to teach him a lesson, but it did not work the way they intended. Sun Wukong defeated them round after round. Finally, he even bested the powerful Heavenly Warrior and his mighty clubs. In a later episode, it takes the intervention of Buddha himself to capture and punish Monkey by imprisoning him under a mountain until he can perform a great service to expiate his crimes. And that is just the beginning of his adventures.

4.18 (facing page)
The monkeys on the Mountain of Flowers and Fruit hoist their king, Sun Wukong, who has returned victorious from his battle with heaven. They proudly fly a banner declaring him 'Great Sage Equal to Heaven.' Hebei Clapper opera

4.19
Sun Wukong easily defeats the Heavenly Warrior and his mighty clubs. Peking opera

Monkey Steals the Magic Fan
三借芭蕉扇
Shaoxing Opera

Sun Wukong got his freedom from Buddha on one condition. He had to join a band of pilgrims on their way to India. Sandy and Pigsy, two other heavenly beings making reparation for their offences, and the monk Xuanzang were all on a mission to get the Buddhist scriptures from India and bring them back to China. While on their way, they came to a scorched land. How were they to cross it? What's more, how were they to pass the great fiery mountain that barred their path?

Monkey learned from the local inhabitants that a fairy called the Iron Fan Princess lived nearby. She had a magic fan that could extinguish the great fiery mountain. Well, said Monkey, that was just the thing. He sought her out and asked as politely as a monkey could for the loan of her fan so that he and his companions could be on their way. The princess was enraged! Monkey was none other than the monster who had once defeated her son in battle. Give him the fan? She waved the fan and conjured up a mighty wind that blew Sun Wukong far away.

Monkey was never one to give up. He returned but this time used his powers to transform himself into a tiny insect. Unbeknown to the princess, he landed in her tea, which she then drank. Once in her stomach, Monkey moved around and about to make her groan with pain. She could only get him to leave her body by promising to give him the fan.

But it was a trick. Monkey soon found out that he had been given the wrong fan. Again he flew back to the princess. If he failed as an

insect, he would not fail as her husband, the Ox King. The unsuspecting princess told the imposter Ox King the whole story of that monstrous Monkey and how she had so cleverly outwitted him. Monkey, as the Ox King, congratulated her and asked for the fan. She gave it to him and guessed only too late that she had been tricked.

The real Ox King returned and managed to get the fan back again. A terrific battle ensued, as the Ox King and Sun Wukong used all their powers and transformations. Monkey triumphed in the end, and the Ox King had to surrender the magic fan. Sun Wukong waved it, extinguished the fire on the mountain, and brought rain to the parched land. The little company of pilgrims was able to continue on its way.

4.20
Sun Wukong rides on Pigsy's back, delighted that he has won the magic fan. He will soon discover that he has been tricked and the fan is counterfeit. Shaoxing opera

4.21 (facing page)
Monkey holds his staff ready to do battle as he seeks out the Iron Fan Princess. Shaoxing opera

Monkey and the White Bone Demon
三打白骨精
Shaoxing Opera

The White Bone Demon was an evil spirit who lay in wait for a special kind of victim. It was determined to get power and immortality by eating the flesh of a holy monk. When the pilgrims approached his mountain, the evil spirit saw its chance. It appeared to the monk Xuanzang as a beautiful young maiden offering to show him the way to a nearby temple. Monkey saw through the disguise at once and wasted no time in killing the maiden with his staff. Xuanzang was furious at what Monkey had done and would not listen to his explanations.

The evil spirit was not dead but took a new form to trick Xuanzang when Sun Wukong was away. This time it appeared as an old woman weeping over the death of her beloved daughter. This, thought Xuanzang, was no doubt the mother of the young maiden whom Monkey had so recklessly killed. To his horror, Monkey suddenly appeared and killed the old woman too. This was evidence that Sun Wukong had not reformed and was not willing to carry out the task of reparation given to him by Buddha. Xuanzang threatened to pronounce secret words – taught to him by Buddha for the purpose of controlling the wayward monkey king – that would cause Monkey intense, unbearable pain.

Monkey was very worried. The monk refused to believe him and was in terrible danger. Sun Wukong had killed mere appearances but not the real demon, who would surely try again. He decided to seek out the demon on his own, and set off to do so. While Monkey was gone, the demon appeared for the third time. Xuanzang saw an old man holding meditation beads in one hand and sutras in the other. The old man complained to the monk that Sun Wukong had murdered both his wife and his daughter. Just

as the disguised demon was taking in the credulous monk, Sun Wukong returned and made to attack the apparition. Xuanzang hastily recited his spell, and Monkey suffered so much pain that the White Bone Demon escaped. Xuanzang lamented that the monkey king was irredeemable and banished him from his company. There was nothing for it but to return to the Mountain of Flowers and Fruit.

Xuanzang, Pigsy, and Sandy finally entered the temple to which the demon had attempted to lure them from the beginning. They felt at once that something was very wrong. Pigsy got out, but before the others could follow the disguise dissolved and Xuanzang saw that he was in fact trapped in a demon's cave.

Alerted by Pigsy, Monkey rushed to his master's rescue. He found a party of evil spirits escorting an old female demon who had been invited to the banquet of monk flesh. Monkey killed them all and by assuming the shape of the old demon gained admittance to the banquet. The White Bone Demon welcomed its guest, unaware of the trick. It showed the disguised Sun Wukong a heated cooking pot and the soon-to-be-stewed captive. Monkey revealed himself and fought the demon until it appeared in its true form of a skeleton and perished. Master and disciple were reconciled, and the pilgrims pressed on westward. But that was neither the end of their adventures nor the last time they would meet demons.

4.22 (facing page)
The White Bone Demon stands surrounded by its armed and fierce fellow spirits. Shaoxing opera

4.23
Xuanzang, duped by the demon, protects what he thinks is an old religious man from the monkey, Sun Wukong. Shaoxing opera

Monkey and the Cave of Spiders
盤絲洞
Peking Opera

Spider spirits inhabited a dark cave deep in the mountains. Like the White Bone Demon, they eagerly anticipated the day when they could feast on the flesh of a holy monk. As it happened, Xuanzang's journey west took him near their cave. The spiders thought him especially delectable. Such a holy man would undoubtedly confer immortality on whomever was clever enough to eat him, and the spiders were determined to be that crafty.

They secured the body of the beautiful Queen of the Land of Women, pulling out her soul and turning her into their creature. She used her charms to entice the monk away from his companions and into the deadly cave of spiders. There, the queen tried to force the monk into a deadly marriage that was to end with an even deadlier wedding feast.

Monkey used all his skills of transformation to gain entrance to the cave and engage the spider spirits in battle. He plucked hairs from his body, blew them into the air, and became not one but many formidable monkeys. After a great battle, in which he defeated the queen, he transformed himself into a chicken and pecked all the spider demons until they were no more. Once again, Sun Wukong had saved Xuanzang and assured that their mission to bring the word of Buddha to China would be successful.

4.24
Pigsy, Sun Wukong, Sandy, and the monk Xuanzang enter dangerous territory on their pilgrimage west. Peking opera

4.25 (facing page)
Sun Wukong uses his skills of transformation to battle the spider spirits, who have secured the body of the beautiful Queen of the Land of Women. He plucks hairs from his body, blows them into the air, and becomes a whole troupe of formidable monkeys. Peking opera

Chapter 5   Emperors and Their Ladies

EMPERORS RULED CHINA from the second century BC to the early twentieth century AD. The Chinese term for emperor was first used by the King of Qin about 221 BC. He united several states clustered around the Yellow River into an empire that was meant to endure forever. Consequently, he took the name First Emperor, becoming Qin Shihuang. It was First Emperor who became famous, or infamous, for the massive forced labour projects that included the Great Wall of China, a network of roads and canals, and a spectacular tomb in Xi'an with thousands of life-sized warriors, horses, and chariots. His dynasty did not endure forever, but emperors ruled China for two millennia after him.

The power of the Chinese emperor was intimately connected with two concepts. The first, that the emperor was the son of heaven, went back to the earliest times, and it meant that he was regarded as the intermediary between heaven and humanity. He was the only one who could perform the necessary rituals and make sacrifices on behalf of the people. The emperor was responsible when heaven was not pleased with the state of the empire and had to prostrate himself in the temple in penance. These practices, descended from the Zhou dynasty kings of 3,000 years ago, continued into the twentieth century with China's final dynasty, the Qing, at the impressive Temple of Heaven, which still stands in Beijing.

The second concept underlying imperial power was that an emperor ruled only with the authority of heaven. His mandate could be revoked if he did not rule well. Ancient philosophers such as Mencius articulated the theory that the emperor was thus obligated by a higher power to rule benevolently for the well-being of all his subjects. An ancient book of history, *Shangshu*, states, 'Heaven sees as far as the people see; Heaven hears as the people hear.' Should the emperor fail to act in the best interests of the people, astrological signs and natural disasters would demonstrate heavenly displeasure, and the mandate would pass to another through insurrection, coup, or invasion. Success or failure was therefore evidence of heaven's will.

The emperors of China gradually became absolute and distant rulers. Elaborate court protocol developed around every aspect of imperial life, so that by the end of the Qing dynasty the emperor was a remote autocrat living in a 'forbidden city.' Yet as the people were cut off from him, so he was cut off from the people. The emperor relied on a vast bureaucratic network of officials to bring him information and to

5.1
Yang Guifei and Emperor Ming, in Reunion in the Moon Palace. *Cantonese opera*

carry out his commands. Princes were made – much as a Western royal would bestow the title of lord. Kings ruled small states, and the emperor ruled a unified country made up of former states.

Emperors, empresses, and imperial concubines have always been a popular focus of traditional Chinese theatre. The following operas bring the audience into the emperors' forbidden chambers to show them and their ladies as idealists, villains, and tragic figures. An emperor might seem remote and godlike in distant Beijing, but he acquires humanity on the stage.

The Intoxicated Concubine
貴妃醉酒
Anhui and Peking Opera

The Intoxicated Concubine is a showpiece for the female role. It is closely identified with the famous female impersonator Mei Lanfang, who is better known in China and the West than any other Chinese opera performer. The role of the concubine requires a range of emotions from joy to sorrow, physical dexterity and lightness to convey drunkenness, and the execution of a particularly difficult arching of the body called a kite turn. Mei Lanfang was able to perform all this in his sixties.

The imperial concubine, known as Yang Guifei, one of the great beauties of China, waited for the emperor. He had promised to come to his favourite in the Hundred Flowers Pavilion, where they would drink, feast, and enjoy each other. She looked for him expectantly, but he did not come. Where was he? A palace eunuch informed her that His Majesty would not come this evening, having gone instead to the quarters of one of his other concubines. Lady Yang was stunned by the news. This was not simply a broken appointment. She was out of favour and had been replaced.

What was she to do? She had been abandoned by the emperor and had lost her status as a consequence. The imperial concubine ordered drink brought to her. She would lose herself in cup after cup. As Lady Yang drank, she became more and more intoxicated until she had to be supported by her maids, who helped her back to her quarters, but the imperial concubine was not finished. She returned to the garden and ordered the eunuchs to bring her more wine. The first eunuch brought the wine, but it was too hot. After cooling it down, he offered the cup to Lady Yang. She looked at it and coyly bent over, hands on hips, picking up the cup with her teeth and arching back-

ward to drink it down. Completely intoxicated, she cast a flirtatious eye at the befuddled eunuch. The second eunuch also brought her wine. Again, she picked up the heated cup with her teeth and drank it down by bending backward.

Alarmed, the eunuchs could think of nothing to do but to make up the story that the emperor had changed his mind and was coming. The maids and eunuchs linked arms in a line on both sides of the imperial concubine to hold her up, but she was still very drunk and when she staggered the whole line swayed

back and forth like a dancing cobra. When the emperor did not arrive, Lady Yang became very angry, slapping one of the eunuchs for refusing to go and command the emperor to come to her. Finally, in a flirtatious mood again, she stole a hat from one of the eunuchs and wore it on top of her elaborate court headdress. Perhaps she would pretend that she was a man! Tiring of this sport, she flung the hat back and staggered into her own rooms.

The emperor, however, did return his attentions – so much so, in fact, that he became infatuated with the beauty and neglected the good government of the empire. Chinese history records that when a rebellion broke out, the emperor's own troops blamed Lady Yang for diverting the emperor and demanded her death. She was strangled with a white silk cord.

5.2 (facing page)
The concubine performs a kite turn to pick up a cup of heated wine with her teeth, drink it, and return it to the tray. Peking opera

5.3
The concubine Lady Yang has drunk too much. Anhui opera

The Emperor's Daughter
帝女花
Cantonese Opera

An emperor of China looked down in sorrow at a young girl. 'My daughter! My daughter!' he cried in anguish. 'Why did you have to be born a princess?' And with that he killed her and took his own life. It was the seventeenth century, and the great Ming dynasty had ruled for nearly 300 years. The imperial household had been planning to celebrate the marriage of Princess Changping to her beloved Zhou Shixian. But the celebration turned to tragedy when the Manchurian tribes of the north invaded China. There was no escape for the emperor or his family. Tradition demanded that the women of the imperial household give up their lives to preserve their honour and that of the dynasty. The emperor gave his daughter a red scarf with which to hang herself, but Zhou Shixian could not bear it and stopped her.

Finally, the emperor himself fulfilled the last duty of a royal house and killed his daughter to protect the family honour. This story tells how suffering touches even an imperial princess and how royalty is bound by its own code.

A court official discovered, however, that the princess was only wounded, not dead. He whisked her off and hid her in his mansion. Once there, Princess Changping began to recover, but she was not safe. The official's son persuaded his father to hand the princess over to China's new rulers and thus secure a position in the new order. Having overheard their plans, the princess escaped with the help of the official's daughter, who had befriended her. Princess Changping assumed the role of a young Buddhist nun who had recently died, and her life was now filled with hard work.

Her drudgery seemed endless, but at least, she thought, she was safe from recognition.

One winter day while she collected firewood, a young man rode by. The princess looked up and panicked. Who was it but her betrothed, Zhou Shixian? But she had been through so much suffering and betrayal. Had he gone over to the enemy? She no longer knew who to trust and so ran into the temple to hide. Zhou Shixian, who still loved the princess, pursued her into the temple and pleaded until she revealed her secret. They did not know, however, that their tearful reunion had been overheard by the mother superior.

In the hope of a generous donation, the mother superior immediately informed the official who had sought to betray the princess that he had been tricked. The official confronted Zhou Shixian and tried to entice him to deliver Princess Changping and cooperate with the new dynasty. They could be married and enjoy life in the palace; the new emperor simply wanted to use her name to justify his throne and stabilize the country. Zhou Shixian knew that neither he nor the princess could escape, so he went to her and argued that they could bargain for a proper burial of her father and the release of her imprisoned brother. Under those terms, the two agreed to give themselves up.

And so Princess Changping and Zhou Shixian returned. The new emperor threw a wedding party for them, welcoming them into the new regime. But the princess and her beloved had other plans. Not wishing to be used by their enemy and having accomplished their goals, the newly wedded couple drank poison and waited beneath a tree in the garden to die. They died knowing that they had fulfilled their duty to the vanquished Ming dynasty.

5.4 *(facing page)*
Princess Changping prepares to hang herself with a
red scarf as the Manchurian invaders enter the
city. Her beloved, Zhou Shixian, cannot endure it
and stops her. Cantonese opera

5.5
Zhou Shixian, wearing his travelling cloak, sees a
Buddhist nun with a familiar face. Cantonese
opera

5.6
The newly married couple, dressed in royal wedding
finery, prepare to drink poison. Cantonese opera

The Emperor's Daughter

5.7
The couple die by poison in the garden rather than serve the new regime. Cantonese opera

'In the Emperor's Garden'
游上林
Yue Opera

An emperor invites his loyal prime minister into an idyllic garden. They speak in poetry of birds and fish, but each word is a disguise. The prime minister is actually the beautiful woman Meng Lijun, who has passed herself off as a man. This is shocking behaviour for any properly brought up Chinese girl, yet it is not the only such story. The most famous is about a maiden, Hua Mulan, who dresses up as a male soldier to take her ailing father's place in war out of the respectable Confucian virtue of filiality. In another story, the maiden Zhu Yingtai dresses as a man so that she can attend a scholar's academy, which is forbidden to women. Interestingly, Hua Mulan did very well on the battlefield and distinguished herself as a warrior, and Zhu Yingtai proved to be an excellent

scholar. In this excerpt from the opera *Meng Lijun*, a woman distinguishes herself by becoming an outstanding prime minister to the emperor. Thus in these stories women who step out of their traditional roles through the device of a disguise find opportunities to excel.

Meng Lijun was a highly educated and beautiful woman, and she attracted the attention of the brother of the emperor's concubine. He competed for her hand in marriage with the young general Huangpu Shaohua but lost. Furious, the concubine's brother arrested and ruined her family, but Meng Lijun narrowly escaped, disguised as a man. Years passed, and one day Huangpu Shaohua arrived at court to receive the emperor's reward for his service on the battlefield. That reward was to be an arranged marriage, but the young man had no room in his heart for anyone but Meng Lijun. To his surprise, the brilliant new prime minister spoke up for the young general and had the marriage put off. Why? Huangpu Shaohua watched the prime minister closely and soon discovered the truth. The prime minister was none other than his beloved Meng Lijun. She would not admit her identity, and so in great hope the general took a portrait of Meng Lijun directly to the emperor. Unfortunately, the emperor was so smitten by the portrait that he decided to trip up his prime minister and win her for himself.

The emperor invited his prime minister into the palace garden to exchange elegant verse. His verse was suggestive, but Meng Lijun did not betray herself. The emperor drew her attention to the fish swimming in pairs in the pond. 'And you and I,' he said, 'our reflections have also been paired like the dragon and phoenix.' The meaning was clear. The dragon

symbolized the emperor and the phoenix represented his mate. Meng Lijun answered, 'Although there are two reflections in the pool, I only see a dragon. I do not see a phoenix.' The emperor complimented his prime minister on his appearance and erudition. 'People say that good fortune comes in the springtime. Don't let the moon shine in an empty cup.' Meng Lijun countered, 'Even if the moon pledges a thousand cups of wine, I see good fortune as ephemeral as a cloud.' And thus she left the emperor, having at least officially preserved her disguise.

Meng Lijun, now alerted that the emperor had seen through her disguise, sought help from the emperor's mother. She heard Meng Lijun's story and reinstated her family. She was now free to admit her identity and marry the young general.

5.8
The emperor and the disguised Meng Lijun, holding their tasselled riding crops, ride in a leisurely fashion through the garden. Yue opera

5.9
*The emperor hints at the truth and tries to trick
his prime minister. Yue opera*

'Wresting the Dragon Throne'
問病逼宮
Sichuan Opera

Not all emperors on the Chinese stage are portrayed as sons of heaven worthy of obedience. It has its Caligulas, too. Succeeding dynasties had a vested interest in vilifying previous monarchs despite their accomplishments. This was the case with Sui dynasty emperor Yang Guang, who ruled China beginning in AD 604. The Sui dynasty itself was very brief, less than forty years. Emperor Yang Guang's accomplishments lie in massive public works. Under his rule, old canals were linked to new ones to build a grand canal system permitting transport of goods between northern and southern China. New roads were pushed out to the frontier, the Great Wall of China was repaired, and enormous grain depots were built up. All of these projects required a great deal of money and labour, which, as with the first emperor, Qin Shihuang, established Yang Guang's reputation as a tyrant. He is primarily remembered for his notorious cruelty and licentiousness, losing the Sui dynasty its heavenly mandate. 'Wresting the Dragon Throne' is a scene from a longer play entitled *Chaos in the Sui Dynasty.* It tells the story of the evil emperor Yang Guang.

Old Emperor Wen lay on his death bed. His son, Prince Yang Guang, came to the emperor's chambers pretending deep concern for his father's health. He expressed his hopes for his father's comfort and quick recovery but in truth was impatient for the old man to die so that he could take the imperial throne. The emperor had a favourite concubine, Chen, who attended him in his illness. Prince Yang Guang fixed his lustful eye upon this great beauty, flirting with her and attempting to seduce her. The emperor was so incensed that he died in a rage.

5.10 (facing page)
The wicked Prince Yang Guang covets the throne.
Sichuan opera

5.11
Prince Yang Guang's face begins to transform into
a mask of evil as his ambition possesses him.
Sichuan opera

Prince Yang Guang then moved aggressively to assume full authority, demanding the crown from his mother at sword point. Knowing him for a monster, she refused. They struggled violently, but the empress was no match for him. She crashed into a pillar and died from the concussion. The new emperor now turned back to the concubine, Chen. Horrified at his attentions, she vigorously resisted him. The new emperor, whipped into a fury, killed her with his own hands.

Other versions of the story do not stop with these bloody deaths. They have Prince Yang Guang killing both his father and an older brother, Yang Yong, to clear his way to the dragon throne. The new emperor proceeds in these versions to kill an official who refuses to issue congratulations to the new monarch. Whatever the truth and whatever the version, Prince Yang Guang, like Cao Cao in *The Romance of the Three Kingdoms*, is remembered as evil incarnate. He was assassinated in AD 618.

5.12
The empress knows Prince Yang Guang for a monster and struggles with him, refusing to give up the crown. Sichuan opera

Death in the Palace
殺宮
Jin Opera

Emperors and wealthy men took concubines. Within the palace or mansion, delicate political tension was played out among these 'small wives,' with the ascendancy of one over another ultimately depending on the favour of the master. How much an imperial concubine could attract, seduce, or dominate an emperor was crucial to her status.

Emperor Yin of the later Han dynasty sat upon his throne and received his concubine Su Yu'e. She had returned from a visit to her father on his birthday, and he had come back with her to offer his gratitude. Her father, Su Fengji, entered the court with thanks and reverence covering up black treachery. He and Su Yu'e had prepared a plot to assassinate the emperor and seize the throne. The first step was to entice the emperor out of the palace. 'I have prepared a great banquet for your majesty,' said Su Fengji. 'Please honour my house by attending it.' The emperor, flattered, agreed to go. The father, smiling in delight, went ahead to make his preparations.

Emperor Yin had another concubine, Liu Guilian, and on hearing that the emperor had accepted the invitation she pleaded with him not to go. She was desperately uneasy, remonstrating with him that an emperor visiting the houses of officials was like water running backward. What was more, history showed that emperors met their ends at the hands of traitors who took advantage of vulnerable situations. Su Yu'e sobbed, complaining of the injustice of these false accusations. The

emperor was displeased with Liu Guilian and distressed at Su Yu'e's tears. He responded curtly that there was no reason not to go.

The concubine's father served a great meal and many cups of wine to his emperor. Suddenly, Su Fengji and his man at arms rushed upon their ruler with drawn swords. The emperor fled for his life, but where was he to go? He was trapped in the mansion of a traitor – but he was not alone. Liu Guilian had commanded General Zhao Pu to shadow him and watch for trouble. Unable to bear staying behind, she too took a sword and went to the banquet, sure that her emperor was in danger. The general slew the man at arms and the concubine fought the traitor herself and defeated him.

Su Fengji was bound and dragged before the emperor, now back on his throne. The court reviled him, and the emperor ordered him led off to execution. But the business of the court was not finished. A palace eunuch brought in concubine Su Yu'e, bound like her father. Concubine Liu Guilian instantly moved to kill her, but the emperor intervened. He listened to Su Yu'e's plea that she knew nothing of her father's plan. Liu Guilian would have none of her lies or artful tears and raised her sword in cold anger, but again the emperor stopped her for now Su Yu'e whispered to him that she was pregnant. Concubine Liu Guilian listened in disbelief as the emperor declared that they must delay punishment. She saw him weaken

5.13
The emperor looks on in alarm as Liu Guilian draws her sword to kill the treacherous concubine Su Yu'e. Jin opera

before Su Yu'e's tearful appeal and tried twice to get him away from her. But each time, Su Yu'e managed to drag him back, gaining more influence over him than before.

Finally, in desperation and fury, Liu Guilian declared that she could help the emperor protect the country only if Su Yu'e were dead. If Su Yu'e lived a moment longer, then concubine Liu Guilian would have to take her own life. The emperor, torn, gave in. Liu Guilian sent him off and raised her sword for the last time to kill the traitorous concubine and her rival.

5.14
Wavering under concubine Su Yu'e's pleas and tears, the emperor restrains the furious Liu Guilian. Jin opera

5.15
Liu Guilian finally kills the traitor. Jin opera

Death in the Palace

The Emperor and the Concubine
順治與董鄂妃
Cantonese Opera

A Cantonese opera premiered in 1989 to considerable interest. It told the story of the first emperor of China's last dynasty. Political intrigue and ethnic tension combined with love and personal tragedy. It climaxed in the dramatic gesture of an emperor of China abandoning his throne in disgust for the beggar's bowl of a Buddhist monk.

The Qing dynasty ruled all of China although its leaders were not Han Chinese but Manchurian. The idealistic young emperor, Shunzhi, wanted to preside over an enlightened reign in which the Han, the Manchurians, and the Mongolians were united as one people. The Manchurian princes, his courtiers, however, thought differently. The emperor chose a beautiful and talented Han Chinese woman, Wu Yunzhu, to be his empress but was overruled by his mother and the princes. It would not do, they argued, to raise a Han so high and leave the Mongolian allies unrewarded for their support. Under their influence, the emperor married Wu Guoying, a Mongolian, and took Wu Yunzhu for a concubine.

The new empress's family was proud and cruel. It used its new status to enrich itself and oppress the people. The emperor learned of this exploitation and was very angry. Determined to change things, he employed the reform-minded scholar Xu Yuanwen to help him heal the empire, but while he turned his eyes outward, he failed to see the evil in his own house. The empress and his beloved concubine both bore him sons, but Wu Yunzhu's was his favourite. The empress's mother, jealous for the power of her house, would not let anyone stand in the way of her family. Her chance came when her grandson became dangerously

5.16
Emperor Shunzhi with his beloved concubine, Wu Yunzhu. Cantonese opera

ill with smallpox. She took a shawl that had
been wrapped around the baby and placed it on
Wu Yunzhu's son. The empress's son recovered, but Wu Yunzhu's died.

The treachery was soon discovered and the
empress's mother was forced to commit suicide.
In a rage, the emperor declared that he would
rid himself of his Mongolian bride and rule
with his first love, Wu Yunzhu. He was also
determined to dismiss the princes as his coun-
sellors and rely on the progressive Xu Yuanwen.
In this, he had gone too far. The Manchurian
princes secretly met the empress's father. This
emperor was much too partial to the Han
Chinese, they argued, and threatened their
power base. He would have to be dealt with.

The princes positioned an assassin by the
Ming tombs where the emperor went to make
ritual sacrifices, with instructions to kill the
emperor on his return from changing into his
ceremonial robes. The hireling watched and
waited. When the emperor returned, the assassin raised his bow and arrow and shot him
with fatal accuracy. The princes moved
swiftly: one killed the assassin to remove the
only witness against them, and the others
quickly declared that as the heir was too
young, they would appoint the empress's father
as regent. But their words died in their mouths
when the emperor appeared on the scene completely unharmed. Who, then, lay murdered
before them? The emperor discovered to his
horror that it was none other than Scholar Xu
Yuanwen, on whom he had pinned so many
hopes. The scholar had taken his place and
died by the arrow meant for him.

At the palace, the emperor's mother told
Wu Yunzhu that an assassin had killed him.
All this trouble had come about because the

The Emperor and the Concubine

emperor had been too partial to the Han to begin with. It was her duty to die with him. Wu Yunzhu, heartsick at the death of her baby son, had already lost the will to live and accepted a silken rope with which to hang herself.

When the emperor returned to the palace and found his beloved concubine dead, his sorrow was complete. He had lost his son, his trusted friend and adviser, and now his beloved. He cried out that his people still suffered, evil princes ruled the country, and there was no justice in the world. He had lost all that was dear to him, and his own sense of sin weighed him down. There was nothing for him in the palace now. He would cut his hair and become a Buddhist monk.

5.17 (facing page)
The emperor tries to console his grieving concubine, who is heartsick at the death of her only child. Cantonese opera

5.18
In despair over the death of his beloved concubine and son, the emperor tries to kill himself with a dagger. Later he abandons the palace for the life of a monk. Cantonese opera

EMPERORS AND THEIR LADIES

Chapter 6   Generals and Warriors

THE MOST FAMILIAR traditional ordering of social classes in China placed the military rank and file close to the bottom of the scale, only marginally better than barbers, entertainers, and prostitutes. Soldiers, after all, were responsible for chaos and misery as one dynasty fell and another arose, although their generals, many of whom became kings, were in a different class. The ordinary Chinese had suffered much at the hands of the military. The ancient practice in the Han dynasty was to make every man eligible for service from his early twenties to his late fifties, requiring him to report for training one month a year and to be constantly ready for a call-up. Military campaigns could take him far from his home and separate him from his family for years. Rivalry between contending states and factions engendered much bloodshed and disrupted stable, civilized life.

Around the sixth century, China began developing a permanent standing army. Every family with more than one son was required to give one up to be a professional soldier. In addition to their military duties, these career soldiers farmed the land to make their garrisons self-sufficient. Large numbers of mercenaries entered the Chinese army, and tribal chieftains were hired to defend China's long and distant borders. Generals and regional commanders oversaw this motley group of soldiers, in the process extending China's empire and consolidating power under one ruler or another. The exploits of many of the great generals, rulers, and strategists – especially during the Three Kingdoms dynasty – became legendary.

The third century in China was a time of violent contention among three prominent states, Wei in the north, Wu in the south at the Yangtze delta, and Shu in the west, where Sichuan province is located today. The events and personalities of that time have indelibly marked China's culture. Stories, plays, and an immensely popular book, *The Romance of the Three Kingdoms,* have kept that time alive in the popular imagination; modern events and contemporary figures are frequently compared to those in the *Romance.*

Liu Bei was the commander of Shu. He swore eternal brotherhood with two valiant men, the impulsive Zhang Fei and the courageous Guan Yu, in a famous episode in a peach grove. Both became legendary generals and later generations would deify Guan Yu. Their enemy was the leader of Wei, General Cao Cao. 'Speak of the devil' is a common expression in the West. In China, people say 'Speak of

6.1
Zhou Yu, in An Auspicious Marriage. *Peking opera*

Cao Cao.' He is the embodiment of villainy in Chinese culture. The state of Wu, led by Sun Quan, allied itself for a time with the enemy state of Shu to defeat the formidable Cao Cao. The *Romance*, the stories, and the plays relate the intrigues and violence of their conflict. The campaigns and battles, the betrayals and the tricks, and the expression of loyal and virtuous sentiments make for a larger-than-life story. These generals mount the stage as giants in Chinese history, literature, and art.

Centuries later, one particular family joined this legendary group as popular subjects of opera and literature. The Yang family produced generations of great generals and warriors who upheld and defended the Song dynasty. Even the servants of the Yang household had reputations for great skill in the martial arts. Their exploits, too, are remembered on the Chinese opera stage.

Stories from
The Romance of the Three Kingdoms

The Changban Slopes
長坂坡
Peking Opera

The figures in the stories of the Three Kingdoms are as familiar in China as King Arthur and the Knights of the Round Table in the West. Westerners share an image of the characters of Merlin, Arthur, and Lancelot. Chinese share an image of the Taoist adept Zhuge Liang and the three sworn brothers of the peach grove, Liu Bei, Zhang Fei, and Guan Yu. Guan Yu, for example, is formidable and intrepid. Actors playing the part of Guan Yu cover their faces with red make-up to express courage. As Guan Yu has been deified, the actors deliberately 'spoil' the make-up with a black mark to avoid offending him with their unworthy impersonation. They carry his characteristic giant weapon, a big blade wielded like a club or an executioner's axe. An especially prominent legendary figure, the character of Cao Cao is classified as a painted-face role. Actors playing General Cao Cao cover their faces in oily white make-up to express evil. They add thin black lines of cunning around their eyes, noses, and cheeks. Liu Bei needed more than just courageous compatriots to fight such a clever and malicious enemy. He needed good counsel and so implored the help of a brilliant strategist, Zhuge Liang. Zhuge Liang was wise in the ways of the world and of heaven. His costume typically displays Taoist emblems reminding the audience that he can read the stars and raise the winds in the cause of good.

General Cao Cao's counsellor brought to his rival Liu Bei an invitation to join forces. The invitation implied a threat, for Liu Bei's troops were hopelessly outnumbered and refusal meant utter annihilation. Liu Bei decided to flee along with his wives, his little son, and all his troops. Cao Cao quickly ordered his great army to pursue them and bring back Liu Bei alive. Liu Bei's forces scattered in confusion. He fled for his life but found himself surrounded by six generals and their troops. 'I surrender,' he lamented. 'The heroes have fallen into fate's trap.' Suddenly, his sworn brother

Zhang Fei appeared with his troops. Zhang Fei, although outnumbered, fought the enemy and barely rescued Liu Bei.

One of Liu Bei's most trusted generals, Zhao Yun, then discovered the commander's second wife groaning in pain. She had been shot through with an arrow while trying to protect the son of Liu Bei's first wife. She entrusted the care of Liu Bei's young son to the general, begging him to bring the boy to his father. Zhao Yun fought bravely on the Changban slopes through enemy lines to accomplish his mission. Cao Cao ordered him caught, and the enemy drove Zhao Yun close to a pit that they had dug to entrap him. But Zhao Yun's mighty horse leapt over the pit and took the general away to safety. Zhao Yun looked into the face of the child and discovered that he had slept through the whole adventure. He delivered the boy to Liu Bei at the Changban bridge, which was then burned to stop the enemy's advance.

6.2 (facing page)
General Zhao Yun, wearing his pennants of command, has put aside his tasselled spear to rest under a tree after a series of battles with General Cao Cao. Peking opera

6.3
General Zhang Fei stands at Changban Bridge ready to protect his sworn brother Liu Bei from Cao Cao's onslaught. Peking opera

Summoning the East Wind
借東風
Peking Opera

Cao Cao's soldiers were brave fighters on land but did not have their sea legs. So when the general moved his fleet down the Yangtze River to the Red Cliff he linked his warships together with iron chains to make them more stable. Zhou Yu, military adviser for the kingdom of Wu, learned what Cao Cao had done and devised a plan to defeat the enemy. Forming an alliance with the kingdom of Shu, the kingdom of Wu would play a daring trick. Grain boats, apparently brought to General Cao Cao by a defector as a gift, would make their way to Cao Cao's fleet. Like the Trojan horse, these boats would actually conceal soldiers. When they were near enough, the lead boats would burst into flames and ram into the enemy, torching the entire fleet. The soldiers would leap into small boats tied to the barge and attack. Four squadrons of warships would come up from behind to press the advantage while armies waited on the roads and in the forest to ambush any who tried to escape.

But there was only one problem with this excellent plan. There was no wind to carry them. And so Zhou Yu fell ill and became melancholy. The Taoist adept and brilliant strategist Zhuge Liang knew the cure. He would use his arts to raise a strong east wind to carry them to victory. He erected a great altar with an elaborate arrangement of flags and costumed soldiers. Standing on its summit, he performed the ritual. As he knew it would, the wind came and carried the boats away to the utter defeat of Cao Cao. A victory, yes, but also the beginning of Zhou Yu's resentment of Zhuge Liang, who now threatened his status as China's greatest tactician.

6.4
Zhuge Liang, dressed in Taoist robes and attended by servants carrying astrological banners, stands before the platform he has erected to summon the east wind. Peking opera

The Huarong Pass
華容道
Peking Opera

General Cao Cao led the tattered remnants of his army and fled for his life to the Huarong Pass. It was very narrow and difficult to manoeuvre through, but it was his only hope. The general was delighted to find it totally undefended. So, the great Zhuge Liang was not so clever after all! Although the great strategist had sent forces to cut off Cao Cao's escape, he had overlooked this route as too improbable. Just as Cao Cao was sure that he had indeed managed his escape his heart froze. He heard the sound of horses. It was the enemy, led by Guan Yu, come to cut him off.

What was to be done? Cao Cao's advisers were all in agreement: they could not hope to fight or to retreat. It was well-known, however, that the imposing Guan Yu was a loyal and honourable man. If they could not escape by arms, perhaps they could escape by playing on his sense of duty and fair play. Cao Cao spoke to Guan Yu and appealed to his memories of an earlier and better time. Had not Cao Cao given him refuge and expensive gifts? Guan Yu had to acknowledge that the general had been good to him and had even once saved his life. Now, this same man stood before him in defeat with a handful of demoralized soldiers. There was a debt to repay and Guan Yu decided to pay it. He lowered his famous blade and ordered his troops to stand aside as Cao Cao fled to safety.

6.5
Guan Yu, in red face and carrying his mighty blade, rushes into the pass to stop Cao Cao's escape. Peking opera

Thus Cao Cao escaped, certain that he had frustrated Zhuge Liang plans to stop him. But the great strategist had read in the stars that Cao Cao's time had not yet come, and so he had deliberately arranged for Guan Yu to guard the way that the general must take. In this way, Cao Cao could follow his destiny, and Guan Yu could repay a debt.

6.6
Holding his riding crop to indicate that he is mounted, Cao Cao has no choice but to appeal for mercy. Peking opera

The Huarong Pass

Memorial to a Rival
臥龍吊孝
Peking Opera

Zhou Yu, adviser to the state of Wu, died in frustration and fury after being bested three times by his arch rival Zhuge Liang. He had lamented to heaven, 'You gave birth to a Zhou Yu, so why did you have to give birth to a Zhuge Liang, too?' The King of Wu was devastated at the loss and ordered a solemn funeral.

Meanwhile, Zhuge Liang, master of the Taoist arts, saw in the heavens that a great star had fallen. He knew immediately that Zhou Yu had died and was determined to go to the enemy state (the brief alliance against Cao Cao having ended) to pay his respects at the tomb. Liu Bei did not want his brilliant adviser to risk his life so foolishly but could not dissuade him. In the end, he sent General Zhao Yun and his soldiers for protection. Zhuge Liang arrived in the kingdom of Wu, mourned at the altar of his rival, and shed many tears. The enemy was so amazed and touched at the noble behaviour of this man that they gave a feast in his honour before letting him return unhindered. Zhuge Liang's recognition of talent and greatness transcended the quarrels of kingdoms.

6.7
Zhou Yu, when alive, was a formidable opponent, as when he plotted the assassination of Liu Bei. Anhui opera

6.8
Zhuge Liang, holding his familiar fan and wearing a cap embroidered with Taoist designs, mourns the death of his talented rival, Zhou Yu. Peking opera

Memorial to a Rival

Cao Cao and Yang Xiu
曹操與楊修
Peking Opera

Cao Cao and Yang Xiu is a modern Peking opera that uses scenery and the intriguing dramatic device of a town crier. The crier appears throughout the play between scenes, shouting out his news and carrying placards that both fit into the action and act as a commentary on it. In this play, the relationship between the jealous, stubborn general and his brilliant strategist ends in waste and tragedy.

Cao Cao had been dealt a terrible blow at the Red Cliffs. He desperately needed talented people to reverse his fortunes. That talent came to him as Yang Xiu, a scholar, who promised to convince another man of talent, Kong Wendai, to come and help too. Cao Cao's army would be strong again in six months or Yang Xiu would personally stand forfeit.

It was clear when nearly six months had passed that Cao Cao's situation was not improving. He had few horses and rations. His remaining troops were grumbling. The general began to drink heavily. One of his officials brought him news that Kong Wendai was in communication with the enemy. Reports had it that the scholar often went in disguise to see tribes from north of Wei, as well as the rulers of Wu and Cao Cao's arch enemy, Liu Bei. Cao Cao flew into a rage at this betrayal. Arrested and dragged before the general, Kong Wendai admitted that he had contacted the enemy. Cao Cao would listen to no more and ordered instant execution.

Yang Xiu, unaware of the execution, met two merchants. One from the north had brought horses while the other from the south had rice. Cao Cao overheard Yang Xiu bargain and threaten until the merchants handed over the desperately needed rations and horses at a

6.9
Misunderstanding the plans of the loyal Kong Wendai, Cao Cao orders his execution. Peking opera

6.10
Yang Xiu, unaware that Kong Wendai is dead,
awaits the traders of horses and rations for the
army. Peking opera

Cao Cao and Yang Xiu

ridiculously low price. He congratulated Yang Xiu but was stunned when the scholar declared that congratulations really belonged to Kong Wendai, who had been busy travelling incognito to make the arrangements. Realizing that he had unjustly killed a loyal and talented adviser, Cao Cao made up a story. Kong Wendai, he said, had entered his room while he was asleep. Cao Cao had jumped up while only half awake and killed him. Yang Xiu was instantly suspicious.

The general buried Kong Wendai with all honours and declared that he would spend a night's vigil at the tomb. During the middle of the night, Cao Cao's beloved wife came and covered him with a cape. Cao Cao was at first greatly moved, then alarmed when he discovered that it had been Yang Xiu's idea. It was a trap to demonstrate that the general did not kill in his sleep. To save Cao Cao from disgrace, the beloved wife killed herself with his sword. Yang Xiu saw through the ruse, and Cao Cao, both embarrassed and angry, gave his daughter to be Yang Xiu's wife as his expression of sorrow.

Some time later, Cao Cao brought his refreshed army west. But it was a cold winter, and Yang Xiu complained that the general had acted against his advice. Even after Cao Cao lost a wager with Yang Xiu over a riddle and acknowledged his cleverness, the general still refused to listen to his counsel. A misunderstanding over yet another appeal to retreat led to Yang Xiu's arrest. The scholar lamented that he had once been free but had lost everything by serving a butcher. Word came that the camp was being overrun by superior enemy forces, but Yang Xiu told the general that he had already given the necessary orders to counter

the attack. Cao Cao's officials pleaded for Yang Xiu, whose wisdom had saved them, but the general was now so jealous that he was intent on killing the adviser. Yang Xiu accused Cao Cao of having long wanted to kill him for having shown up the general. When it was learned that the general's daughter had killed her baby and herself so that she could accompany her husband, Cao Cao delayed no longer and ordered the faithful Yang Xiu's head cut off.

6.11

The generals plead with Cao Cao not to execute Yang Xiu. Peking opera

Burning the Camps
火燒連營
Hebei Clapper Opera

Terrible news came to Liu Bei and Zhang Fei. Their sworn brother, the valiant Guan Yu, had been captured and put to death in the state of Wu. Zhang Fei, inconsolable, mercilessly pressed his troops forward to take his revenge. He ordered two of his officers to prepare mourning garb for the entire army within three days or die. Seeing no way out, the officers mutinied and assassinated him while he slept. They took his head and defected to Wu.

Liu Bei was now alone; he had lost his two sworn brothers of the peach grove. Zhuge Liang advised him that the prudent thing to do was to form an alliance with Wu against their common and more dangerous enemy, the state of Wei. Liu Bei could think of nothing but exacting payment for the death of his compatriots. He attacked the state of Wu with the full force of his army. Guan Yu's son, dressed in white, the Chinese colour of mourning, sought out the enemy general who had been responsible for capturing his father and delivering him over for execution. He pursued the general to a farmhouse in a village. Just as the general was about to make his escape he was startled by an apparition, the spirit of Guan Yu. Guan Xing, the son, took quick advantage and killed him.

Liu Bei's attack was having success, and the state of Wu decided to sue for peace and an alliance against Wei. The sign of sincerity was a gift: the head of Zhang Fei, brought by the two assassins who had killed him. The gift did not reconcile Liu Bei to Wu but rather deepened his sorrow and anger. After executing the assassins, he built a memorial to his two dead brothers and continued the attack.

The enemy general, Lu Xun, retreated, drawing Liu Bei's forces after him. It was a

scorching summer, and Liu Bei's forces decided to make a series of camps in the woods. But the last remaining brother of the peach grove did not listen to his generals, failing to send a map of his troop deployment to his adviser, Zhuge Liang. General Lu Xun saw his chance. He sent his troops into the woods to set fires at strategic locations until all the camps were ablaze. Zhuge Liang heard of the disaster and hastily sent Zhao Yun to rescue the defeated Liu Bei before it was too late. Liu Bei was broken and took to his death bed after the loss of his army, Zhang Fei, and Guan Yu. He committed his son into the care of his great adviser, Zhuge Liang, and died.

6.12 (facing page)
Liu Bei holds a memorial tablet and mourns the deaths of his sworn brothers of the peach grove pact. Hebei Clapper opera

6.13
General Zhao Yun arrives to rescue Liu Bei from disaster. Hebei Clapper opera

Valiant Women

The Chinese opera stage boasts many examples of women warriors. They can handle a variety of weapons, ride horses, and engage the enemy in hand-to-hand combat. Unlike the refined ladies of the women's quarters, these operatic characters do not execute delicate gestures with water sleeves or cross the stage with a mincing walk. Instead, they twirl spears, brandish swords, and fend off attacks with acrobatic prowess. These women can hold their own with male warriors and even best a general. They can, in fact, even become great generals themselves.

Although they do not fight on the battlefield, wives of generals and warriors can also display fortitude, resourcefulness, and courage. In one famous Peking opera, *The King's Farewell to His Concubine*, the heroine resolutely takes her own life so that her king will be able to fight unhampered by worry for her. Such women are models of loyalty and duty. Often, when their husbands do not know where to turn, these women have the answers.

Yang Paifeng Accepts a Challenge
孟良搬兵
Jiangxi Opera

Madam She, the matriarch of the great Yang family of generals, was worried. She had lost her husband, a great general in the service of the Song empire, who died fighting the enemy on the battlefield. Now, she might have lost her grandson, Yang Zongbao, too. General Meng Liang had escorted her grandson behind enemy lines to pay his respects at his grandfather's grave, but why had they not come back? Meng Liang finally returned with bad news. The enemy had discovered them and captured her grandson; Meng Liang had broken through only to come for reinforcements to win him back. Alas, the guard at Madam She's mansion was not up to such an endeavour. How could he solve the problem?

A servant girl of the mansion, Yang Paifeng, decided that she wanted to help. There was more to her than met the eye. She practised swordplay daily and yearned for an opportunity to prove herself. She brought tea to Meng Liang, planning to goad him into noticing her and making use of her special talents. She asked him his rank, and he retorted that he held the highest military rank. On the contrary, insisted Yang Paifeng, failure to bring Yang Zongbao home showed him to be merely ordinary. Affronted, the general took the uppity servant girl to Madam She, who made her kneel in reparation of the insult. Meng Liang declared in his cavalier fashion that unattractive women like Yang Paifeng often do odd things. The servant girl immediately countered by reminding him of the important contributions of a talented former empress, who was plain herself. It was all a question of talent.

Stung, Meng Liang challenged Yang Paifeng to show evidence of her supposed talent. She retorted that her arts were military and that she did not need all the weapons men used to prove it. She picked up a burning stick from the kitchen fire. That would be enough for a challenge fight with the general. The fight began, and the smug general quickly grew alarmed. She was a very skilful warrior and almost killed Meng Liang in the contest as she artfully brandished the stick. Madam She declared that since the servant girl had demonstrated her skills, she should indeed lead a rescue for her grandson. General Meng Liang could only agree that superior ability deserved its chance.

6.14 (facing page)
The clever and able servant girl Yang Paifeng taunts the great general Meng Liang for his failure to rescue his charge. Jiangxi opera

6.15
General Meng Liang discovers that there is more to the servant girl than he expected. Jiangxi opera

6.16
Yang Paifeng hoists her weapon ready to show her military skill. Jiangxi opera

Yang Paifeng Accepts a Challenge

The Warrior Maiden Mu Guiying
穆桂英下山破陣
Peking Opera

The great Song dynasty had become weak. It was constantly threatened by the forces of Liao, from the north. The Liao tribe had a particularly effective military strategy called Heaven's Gate, which had so far proved unbeatable. Any attempt to break through it meant disaster and capture. Something had to be done.

The answer came from the great Yang family, which had produced generations of generals for the Song dynasty. General Yang, the sixth son of the great founding general of the Yang family, knew of a great weapon called Dragon Slayer, kept in the fortress of a bandit king. This weapon was the key to breaking Heaven's Gate. So he sent his only son, Yang Zongbao, to attack the fortress and win the legendary weapon for the Song army. Neither father nor son anticipated the match they would meet in the fortress's guardian.

The bandit had put his daughter, Mu Guiying, in charge of the fortress. She was a fierce and skilful warrior who loved hunting and often rode out to shoot wild geese. While in the forest tracking down a goose she had just shot down, Mu Guiying came across two Song generals. She engaged them in battle and roundly defeated them. They scurried away to report to Yang Zongbao, who was preparing to attack the fortress. He responded quickly by going to meet this formidable female fighter. Mu Guiying, totally confident of her abilities, fought the young general one on one. As the battle continued, she became more and more impressed with the young man and decided that such a warrior would make a fine husband for herself.

She ended the battle, completely defeating Yang Zongbao. If he wanted his freedom he had to agree to marry her. What choice did he have? Yang Zongbao decided to make a condi-tion, declaring that he would wed Mu Guiying if she joined forces with the Song to attack the Liao and break through their famous Heaven's Gate strategy. She agreed, and they solemnized their marriage in the traditional way by bowing to heaven and earth and announcing their intention to wed.

Yang Zongbao returned to camp first while Mu Guiying assembled her forces. Yang Zongbao's father, General Yang, was furious at the disgrace his son had brought on the family. How could he marry a bandit's daughter?! General Yang was about to kill his son in a rage when two things happened. First, the general's mother interceded for her grandson, and second, Mu Guiying and her troops arrived. With his mother's intercession on the one hand and the formidable force of Mu Guiying on the other, General Yang had no choice but to accept her into the family. Mu Guiying now became one of the great generals of the Yang family and prepared to lead the army into battle against the Liao forces.

When the armies of Song and Liao met on the battlefield, General Mu Guiying was pregnant. As the battle began she gave birth to a son, an event hailed by everyone as a sure sign of victory. That day, the Song forces did the impossible and broke through the formerly undefeated Heaven's Gate.

6.17
The couple is happy after Yang Zongbao's father, the commander of the Song army, grudgingly accepts the bandit's daughter into his family. Peking opera

The Warrior Maiden Mu Guiying

6.18 (facing page)
Mu Guiying, dressed as a commander with pennants of command on her back, hunts wild geese with her bow and arrow. Peking opera

6.19
Early in the story, the young general Yang Zongbao does battle with the beautiful warrior maiden, unaware that she is taken with him. Peking opera

Twice-Locked Mountain
雙鎖山
Longjiang Opera

Liu Jinding and her father, a bandit chief, were in hiding on Twice-Locked Mountain. Her skills in the martial arts were incomparable. Her father was concerned that in living their kind of life she would never find a suitable husband, and he determined to arrange a marriage for her. Liu Jinding was unwilling to submit to an arranged marriage, however, declaring that she could handle the affair herself. Her father gave her a hundred days. If she failed to find a proper match in that time, he would arrange one for her.

General Gao Junbao came riding through the mountain pass, leading his men on a mission. His father had been captured by an enemy state and had to be rescued. Liu Jinding saw him and knew that this was the man for her. She set up a placard announcing that they were destined to marry. When Gao Junbao saw the placard, he was annoyed at its effrontery and promptly smashed the offending object to bits. Liu Jinding led out her fighters and challenged the general for having invaded their territory and destroyed her property. A fierce

battle followed, and Liu Jinding's admiration for him grew round after round. Her skills prevailed, however, and the young general found himself captured and bound.

She declared her willingness to marry her defeated opponent, but he would not hear of it. The idea was preposterous. It was unseemly for a general like him to marry such a woman. Liu Jinding decided to take Gao Junbao up the mountain with her and try to convince him back at her camp. She offered to go with him on his rescue mission to save his father, if only

he promised to marry her. Still he refused. Finally, she painted a beautiful picture for him and wrote a poem on it declaring her sentiments. Gao Junbao was startled with her exhibition of talent. This woman was not only skilled in the arts of war but in the literary arts as well. He began to look at Liu Jinding in a different light and decided that it would be a good match after all. He promised to wed her and the two proceeded to complete his rescue mission.

6.20 (facing page)
The warrior woman Liu Jinding leads out her fighters. Longjiang opera

6.21
Liu Jinding engages the young general in battle and is pleased with what she sees. Longjiang opera

6.22
Liu Jinding reveals that she is more than just a good general. Longjiang opera

Twice-Locked Mountain

Princess Baihua
百花公主
Peking and Anhui Opera

Mongolians invaded China in the thirteenth century, toppled the great Song and set up the Yuan dynasty. They were deeply distrustful of the Han Chinese and preferred foreigners for official posts. Many resentful subjects longed for the return of the Song. One of them was Lord Anxi, who lived in the ancient western capital Chang'an, now called Xi'an. Lord Anxi was determined to raise a force to topple the invaders but did not know that his plans had already been sabotaged. The Yuan authorities had sent an infiltrator – who went under the name of Hai Jun – to find out exactly what was going on.

Hai Jun quickly made himself so invaluable to Lord Anxi that another official became both jealous and suspicious. A trick to trap Hai Jun in the bedroom of the lord's daughter and thus bring him into disfavour backfired. At first prepared to kill the intruder, Princess Baihua fell in love with Hai Jun. She was a superior martial artist and presented Hai Jun with one of a pair of twin swords as a love token. Their engagement was sealed.
Yuan forces arrived at the scene to put down the rebels. Princess Baihua led her father's forces out to meet the enemy, but the enemy seemed to know their strategy, the terrain, and

their tricks. Hai Jun's information permitted the Yuan army to ambush and utterly defeat the rebels. Hai Jun, no longer needing to protect his identity, revealed himself and killed Lord Anxi, using the sword given to him by Princess Baihua. He then hunted for the princess and killed her sister. In a rage at the betrayal, Princess Baihua engaged Hai Jun in combat and killed him. The princess lamented that she had not seen clearly enough and blamed herself for the disaster that had come upon them all. Her sister and her father were dead. Their plans were in ruin. In her distress, she drew her sword and took her own life.

6.23
The princess prepares to kill Hai Jun, who has been tricked into entering her private room. Peking opera

6.24
Princess Baihua, after killing the false Hai Jun in
battle, draws her sword to take her own life.
Anhui opera

Princess Baihua

Death at Prayer
吳漢殺妻
Hebei Clapper Opera

Grand General Wu Han returned in triumph to his mother. He had just captured the emperor's rival, Liu Xiu. This would mean even more honours for his already brilliant career, which included wealth, position, and marriage to Emperor Wang Mang's daughter, Lady Nanning. His mother's reaction came as a complete surprise. She berated him, telling him to release his prisoner, cut down the flag marking his official status, and kill his own wife. The general was struck dumb as his mother recounted the family history.

Emperor Wang Mang had taken the throne from the Han dynasty and forced the last emperor to drink poison. Wu Han's father, loyal to the Han, was unwilling to cooperate with the new order and so Wang Mang ordered his execution. The new emperor had only arranged Wu Han's marriage to his daughter in order to protect himself in case the family sought revenge. This Liu Xiu, whom Wu Han had captured, was of the royal house of Han, for which his father had given his life. Wu Han was, his mother insisted, bound by filiality to cut his ties with Wang Mang and exact revenge.

Wu Han prepared to carry out the duty his mother imposed upon him. He was deeply troubled, however, because he loved his wife. Lady Nanning was a devout woman who offered up prayers every day in a Buddhist chapel in reparation for her father's sins and for her mother-in-law's long life. Wu Han came to her, but she would not admit him until he assured her that he had carried out the filial duty of first visiting his mother on his return home. Wu Han told her of his success and of his mother's three commands. She saw that there was no way out and regretted that after

her death there would be no one to pray in the chapel or to take care of his mother, and that she had not borne him any children. The Lady Nanning would submit and asked only that she be given a good burial in a well-marked grave. Wu Han could not bear to kill this good woman, and so to spare him she took up the sword and killed herself.

It now remained for Wu Han to take his wife's head to his mother as proof that he had obeyed her. At first he was unwilling to produce it as it might frighten her, but his mother insisted. When Wu Han's mother saw the head and learned how obedient her daughter-in-law

had been, she cried tears of sorrow.

But what now of Wu Han himself? He declared that his first duty was to take care of his mother; anything else would have to wait. His mother realized that she herself was the last impediment. Only when she was gone would Wu Han be free to join the Han forces and seek revenge. She sent her son away on the pretext of wanting tea, and while he was gone she hanged herself. On discovering what she had done, Wu Han sent his troops away and torched the mansion. He had no more ties to Wang Mang. His family and his home were gone. He left to join the emperor's enemies.

6.25
To spare her husband, Lady Nanning takes up his sword and kills herself. Hebei Clapper opera

6.26 (next page)
Earlier, General Wu Han just cannot bear to kill his good wife, Lady Nanning. Hebei Clapper opera

Prince Lanling
蘭陵王
Hebei Clapper Opera

One of the many distinctive features of Chinese opera is make-up. The painted-face role in particular uses an extraordinary range of colour and design to convey dramatic information to the audience. It is a mask painted directly on the actor's face, defining and delimiting the role. The often-told story of Prince Lanling, however, prefigures the use of the make-up mask on the Chinese stage.

Kingdom contended with kingdom in the fractured Southern and Northern dynasties period. Out of one these kingdoms, Qi of the North, came the story of a prince who used an unusual strategy on the battlefield. Prince Lanling was an intelligent warrior. He was also tall and handsome – entirely inappropriate for

the battlefield. How could he frighten the enemy with such good looks? A warrior needed to strike terror into enemies and put them at an immediate disadvantage. The prince was a good fighter but certainly not terrifying. When fierce soldiers from the kingdom of Zhou attacked, the prince fought valiantly but was not able to resist the invasion and rout the enemy.

The prince's wife, however, was a clever woman with a perfect solution. She presented him with a shockingly horrible mask. All he needed to do was don the mask before a battle to paralyze the enemy with his dreadful appearance. From that time on, Prince Lanling was even more successful in war than before.

The demonic mask always put his opponents to rout.

His soldiers celebrated their victories and their great commander by performing a dance in which they imitated the prince frightening whole armies with his wife's mask. The king became jealous of Prince Lanling's successes and worried that the courtier prince might become so great in the eyes of his soldiers that he threatened the throne. Only one thing could be done. When an enemy army of a hundred thousand men attacked, the king seized his chance. He ordered the prince to meet the invader but gave him only five hundred men to carry out his mission. Surely this would be the end of the charismatic prince.

The king was not pleased to see the prince return in victory having won even more glory for himself. Mad with jealousy and fear, the king continued to wait for an opportunity to rid himself of his rival. Finally, he gave poisoned wine to the prince. Prince Lanling knew it was poisoned, but drank it down to prove his loyalty. Having survived the attacks of thousands in battle, he died at the hands of his own king.

6.27
Prince Lanling, a formidable fighter, engages attacks from both front and behind. Hebei Clapper opera

Prince Lanling

6.28 (facing page)
The handsome Prince Lanling strikes a pose in
battle. Hebei Clapper opera

6.29
Prince Lanling wears the mask his wife fashioned
to frighten the enemy. Hebei Clapper opera

Chapter 7   *Scholars and Officials*

In China scholars and officials were closely identified with one another for nearly two millennia. Imperial China developed an examination system designed to identify and promote talented men, who helped the emperor to administer the empire. Thus officials who had emerged through a demonstration of academic excellence were used in place of the aristocracy by blood found in the West, and their status could not usually be passed down through the family. In fact, appointments had time limits, and one maintained rank only at the pleasure of the emperor or local governor.

Theoretically, exams were open to anyone from any level of society, and it is clearly evident in Chinese drama that the system did permit some social mobility. The Chinese stage offers many plays in which poor scholars go off to the capital, perform brilliantly on the exams, and win official appointments. Audiences were used to this turn of events as a dramatic device around which a writer would weave certain themes.

Success at examinations meant a degree and the opportunity for a career as a civil servant. As the main route to prestige, the examination system fostered a culture in which the scholar was respected above all others and encouraged the educated to use their knowledge in governance of the country. But learning was primarily literary, centring on the Confucian classics. Scholars were assessed for their erudition, elegant essays, and superior calligraphy.

The empire gained durability from the entrenchment of scholar-officials whose sense of history and devotion to the classics made them a powerful conservative force. Emperors did not have to rely on men of little or no talent whose only claim to authority was a family name. Yet they found themselves increasingly dependent on educated civil servants who could effectively delay or obstruct an edict or government program that they did not fully support. In the West, Plato advocated that philosophers be entrusted with governance, though of course this never happened. In China, the day-to-day running of an empire was in the hands of scholars.

7.1
Lu You, in The Poet Divorces His Wife. *Yue opera*

Judge Bao's Apology
包公賠情
Yue Opera

Sherlock Holmes was Victorian England's relentless agent of justice. Incorruptible, indefatigable, and tenacious, he used observation and reason to expose villainy and rescue the innocent. Judge Bao Zheng performs this role in China, but unlike Sherlock Holmes he was not the invention of a writer. Bao Zheng lived in the eleventh century. His reputation comes down to us through plays and stories that hold him up as a model of justice. He was not impressed by official position or wealth, and he did not look down on poverty or low status. His main preoccupation was with the truth. If the Chinese audience of the Judge Bao plays could not find impartial justice in real life, it could find its ideal on the stage. There, wrongs were redressed and villainy properly punished, no matter how high or how wealthy the villain might be, no matter that the criminal might be the judge's own relative.

Once there was a terrible famine in the countryside. The emperor entrusted Judge Bao Zheng with a mission to distribute food and relief to the disaster victims. He set out immediately. Along the way, however, a crowd of common people pressed onto the road with petitions. What was this? What could they want? They protested that Judge Bao Zheng's own nephew, Magistrate Bao Mian, was corrupt and exploiting the people. One complained that he extorted money from them, another that he killed whomever and whenever he pleased. Yet another told of how the magistrate expropriated grain for his own use. The people appealed to Judge Bao Zheng for help in their misery. The judge ordered the magistrate to be brought before him in the street. He confronted his nephew with the accusations, and the people presented their evidence. The case

against him was irrefutable, and the magistrate confessed his wrongdoings. Judge Bao Zheng sentenced his nephew to immediate execution.

After the execution, the judge went straight to Lady Wang Fengying, his sister-in-law and Magistrate Bao Mian's mother. She had taken care of Judge Bao Zheng and raised him for eighteen years. He paid her the filial respect due to a mother. The judge told her the story, and as her face drained of all colour informed her that the execution had already been carried out. The judge apologized for causing her pain, but stood by his decision.

The evidence was as unassailable as a mountain, he said, and the decrees of justice were just as immovable. In sorrow and rage Lady Wang Fengying grabbed a sword to slay the judge. Yet she faltered as she heard him declare that the law must not be applied with a double standard. If he had freed her son, would he not also be guilty of oppressing the people and betraying the emperor's trust? Lady Wang Fengying was moved by his dedication to impartial justice, his country, and the people even over his own family. She lowered her sword and forgave him.

7.2
The upright Judge Bao Zheng tells his sister-in-law that he ordered the execution of her son. Yue opera

7.3
Lady Wang Fengying raises a sword in sorrow and rage. The judge explains that impartial justice takes precedence even over family. Yue opera

The Prime Minister of Wei

相國志

Shaoxing Opera

China broke into several states loosely linked to the Zhou court between the seventh and fourth centuries BC, called the Spring and Autumn Period. *The Prime Minister of Wei* is set in these times. The opera shows how personal honour and loyalty to one's country take precedence even over family relationships. It is also a story of faith. A prime minister pledges all that he has because he believes in the integrity of one man, a man capable of disowning his own son because the son has dishonoured his family by betraying his country. The king, who has the power to hand out rewards for service, learns that integrity is above wealth and position.

The court of the kingdom of Wei was faced with terrible news. The country had been invaded. The king declared that a worthy general must be selected at once to fight off the enemy. But who should it be? The loyal prime minister of Wei, Zhai Huang, counselled the king to appoint the prime minister's own retainer, Yue Yang, a talented and intelligent man. The king was hesitant to do so, and the king's uncle, Wei Li, was adamantly against the idea. After all, there were stories that Yue Yang's own son had gone over to the enemy years ago and was now a high official. How could a father be expected to fight resolutely against his son? While the king considered what to do, his uncle obtained proof that Yue Yang's son had secretly crept into the city with a letter from the king of their enemies offering his father wealth and position if he would defect as his son had done.

Yue Yang was outraged at the disgrace his son had brought to the family name. Although his son had escaped, he offered the king a pledge written in blood to defeat the enemy

within three months. The prime minister of Wei urged the king to trust Yue Yang and offered up himself, his family from the youngest to the oldest, and all that he possessed as a guarantee of his retainer's loyalty. The king agreed to appoint him, noting that there was no one else capable of carrying out such an important commission.

Yue Yang led the army against the enemy, but the situation was poor. His troops were not properly prepared, and rations were low. There was not enough money even with a large personal donation from the prime minister. Yue Yang decided on a stratagem. He called off the attack and ordered a retreat. Secret messages sent to the enemy stated that Yue Yang was now interested in talking to his son about his proposal. Meanwhile, the court of Wei heard that its general had halted the attack, retreated, and made overtures to the invaders. It seemed he had defected. The king in a rage rescinded Yue Yang's authority and reminded his prime minister of his guarantee. It was the official's seventieth birthday. His family dutifully paid its respects, one by one turning themselves in.

Word came to Yue Yang that the enemy had sent out troops for an attack elsewhere. Now was his chance. The Wei troops were rested and ready; the enemy was unsuspecting. Yue Yang's son came as invited to meet his father with his wife, an enemy princess. He was shocked at his reception. Yue Yang berated his son as a traitor and sent him away, declaring that he was no longer part of his family. Yue Yang was on the point of pressing his advantage when the king's uncle arrived and demanded that he hand over his seal of authority. The captains attempted to defend their

7.4

A eunuch holds up the scroll on which the prime minister writes his guarantee. Shaoxing opera

commander, but the uncle would not hear them. Yue Yang handed over the seal and left the camp.

Moments later, the prime minister arrived with news that the king had changed his mind. It was clear from the captains and soldiers that Yue Yang was no traitor but a careful and clever strategist. The king's uncle was not convinced until, suddenly, soldiers brought in a stew made from the body of Yue Yang's son. It was a 'gift' from the enemy to Yue Yang for having refused to betray his country.

The king arrived and with his prime minister searched for the wronged Yue Yang outside the camp. But once the commander was found he proved unwilling to take back the seal of authority, believing that he had been doubted too many times. The king promised riches and position after the defeat of the enemy. At this, Yue Yang made to leave without a word. The prime minister hastily explained to the king that Yue Yang was a great man who did not serve for riches or honours. What then, asked the exasperated king, did he want? The prime minister said simply 'trust.' The king understood, tore up the blood letter saying that he needed no such guarantee any longer, and put his confidence completely in Yue Yang to serve the state selflessly. Yue Yang took back command and went on to lead the army of Wei to complete victory.

7.5
Far outnumbered by the enemy, Yue Yang calls a retreat, forcing his horse to rise and go on. Shaoxing opera

7.6
The prime minister is distraught that Yue Yang has left the camp. He flings his beard about in his anxiety and hastens to find him. Shaoxing opera

The Prime Minister of Wei

Jing Ke, the Loyal Assassin
荊軻
Cantonese Opera

The story of Jing Ke is one of China's most famous. The great historian Sima Qian recorded the event more than 2,000 years ago. It has told countless generations about courage and sacrifice. The deed that it recounts was not successful, but that does not seem to matter. Jing Ke's gesture is worthy of remembrance and holds a special place in the literary, theatrical, and visual arts.

A talented and educated scholar who loved study and swordsmanship settled in the ancient state of Yan. His name was Jing Ke. His was a particularly violent time. The many states warred with each other and one, the state of Qin, threatened to swallow the others. One of the generals of Qin, who had incurred the displeasure of his king, defected to the state of Yan and nursed a grudge, waiting for revenge. The opportunity came soon.

The Prince of Yan watched with alarm as Qin expanded its power. It was clearly only a matter of time before it would reach its greedy hands into his kingdom. The prince resolved to stop the king who wished to make himself first emperor of all. His plan was not an honourable one, but the times were desperate: he would send an assassin in the guise of an ambassador suing for peace. The prince heaped honours and position on Jing Ke, prevailing upon him to accept the heavy and undoubtedly fatal responsibility of assassin. Jing Ke finally accepted.

He could not go to the court of the careful and suspicious Qin king empty handed. The Qin general who had defected knew exactly what would work, and offered Jing Ke his own head – an acceptable sacrifice for revenge – to make the king believe that the state of Yan slew his enemies for him. The Prince of Yan gave Jing Ke a map of Yan territory to offer to the enemy. Its real purpose was to conceal a poisoned dagger. The crown prince and his courtiers wore white, the colour of mourning, as they escorted Jing Ke to the river. There was much sadness and many tears. Jing Ke faced them all and sang, 'Winds cry and the river waters are icy. A brave man goes but can never return.'

7.7
The Prince of Yan and the courtiers accompany Jing Ke to the river, where he must go on alone. Cantonese opera

The loyal assassin arrived at the Qin king's court. He obtained his audience, presented the severed head, and drew out the map. Quickly, he seized the king's sleeve and lashed out with his dagger. The king broke away, but Jing Ke pursued him around the throne room. The courtiers were in complete disarray. Arms of any type were forbidden in court to anyone except the king, and no one came forward to help. Finally, the king drew out his own sword. Jing Ke, seeing that he had lost the advantage, threw the dagger in the blind hope that he might even then accomplish his mission. He missed, and by now the palace guards had reached them. Wounded, he leaned against a pillar, cursing the ambition of the king. The guards closed in and killed him.

7.8
The King of Qin eagerly examines the map while Jing Ke snatches out the dagger concealed at the end of the scroll. Cantonese opera

7.9
Having drawn his sword, the king defends himself from the assassin as the courtiers are left in confusion. Cantonese opera

7.10
The palace guard pins Jing Ke against the pillar, where he prepares to die. Cantonese opera

The Ode to Constancy

白頭吟

Yue Opera

The story of Sima Xiangru and Zhuo Wenjun is one of China's favourite romances. A Chinese audience will anticipate the much-loved scene of the poor scholar and the beauty who abandoned her riches for him and opened a wine shop to survive.

Talented musician and master of the literary arts, Sima Xiangru attended a banquet at the home of a wealthy merchant. The merchant did not appreciate the young man's talents, but his recently widowed daughter, Zhuo Wenjun, did. Sima Xiangru played a famous love song for her on the zither, which touched her heart. After returning home, he summoned all his poetic skills and composed a love letter, sending it to her the next day. Zhuo Wenjun's father, unaware of the developing romance, had been busy making plans. He was without a male heir to his fortune and had hit on a solution. He would arrange the marriage of his nephew to one of his two daughters. In fact, his nephew and younger daughter were in love and hoping to marry, but it was unseemly that the younger daughter should marry while her sister remained single. The father would therefore announce a marriage between his older daughter, Zhuo Wenjun, and his nephew.

Zhuo Wenjun implored her father to change his mind, but he would not hear of it, dismissing scholars and poets out of hand. It was not worth the effort to study; there was many a poor scholar in the world. Unable to dissuade him, Zhuo Wenjun resolved to elope. It was the only way to preserve her happiness as well as that of her sister and cousin. When her father discovered that she had run away, he declared that she was no longer a daughter of his house.

The two lovers lived in marital bliss but

dreadful poverty. The talented scholar, without employment, dreamed of making his way to the capital and offering his services to the emperor. The emperor appreciated a man of letters, but how could Sima Xiangru afford to reach him? At first he hoped that a dowry would accompany Zhuo Wenjun. When it did not, the couple had to rely on their own resources, selling the jewellery and effects that Zhuo Wenjun had brought with her and opening a wine shop. Word of this made its way back to Zhuo Wenjun's father, who could not abide the disgrace and still had a tender spot for his daughter. He sent a dowry so that the couple could be free of their indignity.

The young scholar now had his chance to rise in the world. He travelled to the capital and was recognized by the emperor as a man of talent. He became an ambassador of the imperial court and was sent away for three years to a distant barbarian land. The new ambassador was very successful; he opened a new transportation route and won good relations for his emperor. He did so well, in fact, that he caught the eye of a beautiful chieftain. Sima Xiangru spent much time with her and rumours began to fly that the two would soon marry.

Zhuo Wenjun's father had business contacts along the transportation route and heard from them that his son-in-law was about to marry a barbarian princess. He went to his daughter with the news, but she would not believe it. She wrote the elegant 'Ode to Constancy,' addressed it to her husband, and sent it by way of a trusted servant.

Sima Xiangru did not know what to do. The chieftain's attentions put him in an awkward position. He certainly did not want to damage the diplomatic relations that he had so

carefully built up. While he mused on his dilemma, Zhuo Wenjun's servant arrived with the letter and scolded him for his apparent faithlessness. Sima Xiangru read the ode and was so moved that he decided to return to his beloved immediately, no matter what the cost. He dreamed of their past and of their future together and sang her ode to constancy. The ambassador set out for home. Zhuo Wenjun and her father stood together at the city gates as her husband, now a great Han official, returned. He had achieved position and honours, but none of it could compare to his love for the merchant's daughter who had left all behind to follow him.

7.11 *(facing page)*
Without a dowry and poverty stricken, Zhuo
Wenjun opens a wine shop. Yue opera

7.12
Zhuo Wenjun and the talented young scholar
Sima Xiangru fall in love at her father's banquet.
Yue opera

7.13
Sima Xiangru, now dressed as a successful official, returns after reading Zhuo Wenjun's 'Ode to Constancy,' and the couple is reunited. Yue opera

The Ode to Constancy

'Death in the Temple'
殺廟
Ping Opera

It is a common practice in Chinese classical theatre to perform excerpted scenes from long plays. The scenes are treasured dramatic moments and often include virtuoso performance pieces. Chinese audiences are thoroughly familiar with the plots of traditional plays and bring to them a lively expectation. The excerpts require no exposition, as the audience has not come to find out what happens but to appreciate the execution of just part of a story. There is thus nothing jarring about a combination of selected scenes presented one after another from diverse plays. 'Death in the Temple,' from the traditional Qin play *The Story of Qin Xianglian*, is one such scene. The scholar in this play is brilliant and talented but utterly without morals. He is the villain of the piece yet never appears. His presence, however, is constantly felt on the stage.

Qin Xianglian brought her daughter and son to the emperor's palace in search of her husband, Chen Shimei. Years earlier, her husband had left the countryside to take the exams that provided a doorway to position and influence. He had done well, so well in fact that the emperor took notice and offered the princess as wife to the new graduate. He agreed, the match was made, and his future was secure.

But then Qin Xianglian appeared with his children in tow. This complicated matters greatly. It was a capital offence for a married man to marry a princess, and Chen Shimei had neglected to tell the emperor about his country family. When Qin Xianglian arrived at his doorstep, he ordered her driven away, feigning ignorance of her identity. She left cursing her heartless husband and his greed for power and wealth. Having nowhere to go, she and her children took refuge in a temple.

In the meantime, Chen Shimei sent a trusted man, Han Qi, to pursue his wife. His orders were to kill the woman driven from his door. Han Qi followed her to the temple, forced his way in, and drew out his knife to slay her. 'Why do you want to kill us?' screamed Qin Xianglian. Han Qi answered that it was the order of his master, Chen Shimei, whom she must have greatly offended. When she discovered that it was her own husband who had arranged the murder, she begged for mercy and told Han Qi her story. She had taken care of her husband's aged parents until they died in the great famine. Then she and her children had made their way to the capital begging for food as they went. But Chen Shimei drove her away. She did not understand. Han Qi, however, did: the emperor's son-in-law had a country wife who could cost him everything. The retainer railed against Chen Shimei, who was worse than a wolf and had sent him to commit such a dishonourable act.

Qin Xianglian offered herself as victim if only he would spare her children. Han Qi clearly saw what lay before him. If he killed her and freed the children, Chen Shimei would surely kill him. If he killed the mother and children, his conscience and heaven would reproach him, and Chen Shimei would kill him anyway to remove any evidence of the crime. If he freed mother and child and ran away himself, the emperor's son-in-law would track him down on some pretext using the resources of the court. There was no place to go and nothing he could do to escape his fate. Han Qi sent Qin Xianglian to the door, and while she was gone killed himself. In this way he would purchase freedom for the wronged woman.

7.14
Han Qi prepares to carry out his orders to kill Qin Xianglian and her children. Ping opera

When she returned and discovered the body, Qin Xianglian swore revenge for this good man, picking up the knife and running out of the temple to seek honest Judge Bao Zheng. There she would find justice. But that is another story.

7.15
After hearing the true story about his master, Han Qi cannot reconcile his conscience with loyalty, and kills himself. Qin Xianglian laments the death of this loyal but conscientious man. Ping opera

'Death in the Temple'

Virtue amid the Flowers
花中君子
Yue Opera

Eunuchs gained much power and influence in the Ming dynasty, which ruled China from 1368 to 1644, and in the process acquired a reputation for greed, duplicity, and scandal. The scholar-official class disliked them for having usurped the functions and place that traditionally belonged to them. In *Virtue amid the Flowers*, it takes an honest scholar-official to set right the wrongs committed by the hated eunuchs.

Liu Jin was a ruthless and powerful eunuch official. He had ruined many an honest man, among them Li Jiusheng, a poor but promising scholar. Li Jiusheng had passed the examinations but had failed to send the necessary bribe to Liu Jin to secure an official's position. Discovering that he had been passed over, he accused the eunuch of corruption. Li Jiusheng was severely beaten for his audacity and eventually died of his wounds. He left a daughter and a son, and they had no one to turn to. The daughter, Li Suping, decided to sell herself into service in order to raise enough money to bury her father properly. Her brother, Li Fengming, went off to fend for himself.

Li Suping soon discovered that she had been sold into a brothel, not into domestic service. Once there, however, she convinced the madam that she was an educated woman. Her father had taught her to read, and she had the extraordinary ability to write with both hands simultaneously. She could handle the books and write poetry that was good enough to sell. The madam tried her out and found her to be as talented and useful as she had said.

Li Suping had made as comfortable a niche for herself as possible but missed her brother. Thinking of him, she took a young boy, Chen Kui, under her care. He was another of Liu

Jin's many victims, who now sold paper and writing materials to the brothel. She encouraged him to study and prepare for the exams. Perhaps one day he would be able to rise above his misfortune. That day was ten years in coming. Liu Jin, the evil eunuch, finally fell from power and was arrested for corruption. Chen Kui took the examinations and passed with the highest honours. He had distinguished himself so greatly that he was made an important imperial official.

At the same time, however, the madam sold Li Suping to a wealthy old man as a concubine. Li Suping resisted until the old man took her to the local court for justice for himself and a beating for her. He made sure to bribe the local magistrate first. The magistrate who was so easily bought was, in fact, Li Suping's brother Li Fengming. He had managed over the years to acquire a minor position and maintained himself through a system of bribery. He had no idea of the whereabouts of his sister. For all he knew, she was a servant somewhere. Li Suping was brought into the court, but neither sister nor brother recognized one another. He ordered her beaten in fulfilment of his bargain, and the punishment was so severe that her hands were covered with blood. It was when he saw that the prisoner could write with both hands at once that he realized who she really was.

Li Fengming cleared the court and revealed his identify. Li Suping was horrified. Their father had died at the hands of corrupt officials. How could he become one himself? She accused him before the new high official, Chen Kui. In deference to her family he was prepared simply to lower Li Fengming's rank but Li Suping would not hear of it. Her brother had

never had the chance of a proper upbringing. The only answer was to strip him of rank and authority completely. She would then take him away to their old home and take charge of teaching him all over again. The new official, Chen Kui, agreed to her request, and she led her brother away to remake his character.

7.16

Li Suping's hands are covered in blood after being tortured for refusing to obey the magistrate's order to marry the merchant. Yue opera

Virtue amid the Flowers

Li Suping demonstrates in court her ability to write with both hands simultaneously. Yue opera

7.18
Li Suping berates her brother for giving in to corruption and misusing his office. Yue opera

Chapter 8   Wealthy Families

Wealthy families in China depended on land. The great landowning families parcelled out their land to be worked by peasants and took a healthy share of the produce. As time went on, they invested in mercantile and moneylending ventures to increase their fortunes. These families were not part of an aristocracy of title and blood. They were great houses because they had great resources. It is not surprising, however, that the gentry class supplied many of China's scholar-officials. Members of wealthy families had the means and leisure to prepare for exams and thus clear the way to official status. Books, tutors, and time were luxuries, after all. The opportunity for such families to enhance their status by providing well-educated candidates for the exams made them powerful supporters of the Confucian tradition.

It was common for several generations and branches of a family to live together in a mansion with gardens and courtyards. Life went on within the walls of these miniature worlds largely oblivious to what was occurring beyond them. Indeed, a woman in a great family would rarely leave her mansion.

Women in traditional China had very clearly defined roles, particularly in the homes of the wealthy. A daughter was required to obey her parents, most notably to accept whatever marital arrangements they made. Such arrangements were made for the prosperity and social position of the family, not for her personal happiness, and the theme of suffering caused by arranged marriages is very old. A wife was expected to obey her husband and to serve his parents. The wicked mother-in-law, like the wicked stepmother in Western fairy tales, is a familiar figure in Chinese stories, a great many of which tell of the sufferings of a young wife with an absent husband at the hands of her imperious mother-in-law. It was only when she became a mother herself, and later a mother-in-law, that the average woman could gain some status and power. But in those stories, her power is primarily wielded over women servants and, of course, her own daughter-in-law.

Great families could and did fall. An indiscretion committed by one distant member of the family could provoke the wrath of the emperor and bring punishment down upon the entire household. Land, position, and wealth could all be lost, as in the opera *Daughters*. Great families were also replaced by new ones at a

8.1
Jia Yuanchun, in The Scenic Garden. *Yue opera*

change of dynasties. New ones continually rose from the merchant class, which gained power through business although on the bottom of the traditional social scale. The Chinese stage presents all these circumstances and gives the audience a close look at the domestic lives of the great.

Daughters
五女拜壽
Yue Opera

Daughters is a modern opera that at first reminds one of Shakespeare's *King Lear.* An old man pays too much attention to his daughters' insincere declarations of undying devotion. He is unable to recognize true devotion because he uses a faulty measuring stick. When his fortunes change he finds himself rejected by those he had believed but cared for by the one whom he had earlier rejected. Like Shakespeare's king, he learns to see through bitter experience. Western audiences might make this literary association, but a Chinese one will make a more immediate connection.

The opera points to that violent and agonizing time between 1966 and 1976 – the Cultural Revolution. Chinese society was turned upside down, as everything and everyone underwent close scrutiny for political orthodoxy. Families were torn apart and friends accused each other. The subtext of the play is that in such circumstances even the time-honoured family relationships cannot be relied on.

Yang Jikang, the head of a great house, turned sixty. A sixtieth birthday was a significant event in China, and so Yang Jikang's family gathered to celebrate. He had five daughters, and, one by one, four of them offered their extravagant gifts, best wishes, and declarations of filiality. They even competed before him for the honour of taking care of him in their own homes. His third daughter, however, had married a poor scholar who had not yet succeeded at the exams. They had little to offer in the way of gifts, so the daughter had embroidered two pairs of shoes. Worse, thieves had stolen these gifts the day before, and she arrived empty handed. Yang Jikang and his wife gave their third daughter a cold reception.

Neither she nor her husband was invited to the great banquet but were sent to the kitchen to eat with the servants.

Shortly after, Yang Jikang and his wife met with disaster. A relative offended a powerful official who had the emperor's ear. Punishment extended, as punishments often did, throughout the family. Yang Jikang lost his position, power, and wealth. His land was confiscated and he and his wife were sent away from the palace with only a maid, Cuiyun, to accompany them. Homeless, they went to their first daughter, who had so ardently competed for the right to shelter him. But her husband was busy building favour in high places. He could not have his investment ruined now by harbouring an enemy of the court. The first daughter turned the old couple away. To his horror, Yang Jikang discovered that each of his daughters rejected him in turn, afraid of offending powerful officials now that he was without means.

Driven from their doors, Yang Jikang and his wife were forced to live on the streets and in old, abandoned temples. Cuiyun accompanied them on the long road to the third daughter's house and cared for them with all her strength. Finally, she collapsed in a snowstorm but luckily was rescued by none other than the third daughter's brother-in-law. A perfect gentleman, he would not dream of touching a young woman with his hands and so bore her on his back to his home. When the daughter learned what had happened, she took them all in without reservation. Both Yang Jikang and his wife were deeply moved at the devotion of their daughter and of their faithful servant. They were ashamed, too, at how they had treated their daughter in her poverty.

8.2 (facing page)
The third daughter embroiders and chats with the maid while her husband, here played by a woman, studies in the Yang family kitchen. Yue opera

8.3
The third daughter's brother-in-law, played by a woman, uses his back to support the fainting maid and thus avoid the impropriety of touching a young woman with his hands. Yue opera

Their son-in-law was not at home; he had gone off to try the exams yet again. Word soon came that he had excelled above the rest and won for himself the highest honours and official titles. With his new influence, he was able to reinstate Yang Jikang to his former position. The older man's lands were returned and all was as it had been.

Yang Jikang's wife now turned sixty and again there was a great celebration. As before, the five daughters appeared with their gifts and best wishes. But Yang Jikang would have none of them and sent the hypocritical four away. He and his wife would celebrate only with his third daughter and with their loyal Cuiyun, whom they now adopted as their own. They had learned that true devotion and sacrifice could only be proven in times of distress.

8.4
Yang Jikang and his wife become beggars, rejected by his daughters and relatives after he loses his position, his wealth, and all his property. Yue opera

Dream of the Red Chamber
紅樓夢
Yue and Huangmei Opera

Dream of the Red Chamber was written more than 200 years ago and is one of China's most famous novels. Young ladies' rooms are 'red chambers.' The novel centres on two young ladies and a young man, Jia Baoyu, who spends his time in a world cut off from the outside. By the end of the novel, the family's fortunes have turned, and they lose their mansion. Everything is vanity, ephemeral, and thus a dream. Audiences in China are thoroughly familiar with the intricacies of the novel's plot as it has been retold on the stage and on the screen many times. The private world of the Jia family is the setting for a drama that continues to touch the imagination.

Baoyu, the much-pampered Jia son, moved into the family mansion's Scenic Garden, a suite of rooms around a courtyard, with his two cousins, Lin Daiyu and Xue Baochai. Lin Daiyu was a fragile young girl who had come to live in the Jia household after her parents died. Xue Baochai, by contrast, was lively and soon became the family's favourite. At first the life of these three together in the Scenic Garden was idyllic. They enjoyed its beauty and wrote poetry to read to one another. Jia Baoyu much preferred this existence to his Confucian studies and preparation for the hateful exams. He wanted to enjoy life and, particularly, he wanted to enjoy the companionship of Lin Daiyu, with whom he had fallen in love.

Father Jia was furious to learn through the servants of how his son wasted his time. He had only consented to the move to the garden because it was a good place to study. He gave Jia Baoyu a severe beating and a strong warning to mend his ways. Lin Daiyu, whose health was weakening, came to see how badly Jia Baoyu was hurt. He put on a brave face and

even sneaked over later to see her because he was concerned about her cough. Only when she was better, he declared, would he be better. He wished he could escape from the confines of the house to live the simple life of a fisher in a beautiful river valley. Were she stronger, she affirmed, she would go with him as his companion.

Lin Daiyu, ill and deep in melancholy, began to see the exquisite garden in a new light. She felt great sadness that all its beauty was so temporary. Blossoms had already fallen, cut by the wind. She did not dare to tread on them, but in her sorrow buried them. She prayed for the souls of the flowers and then wondered who would do so for her. Jia Baoyu

saw what she did and was deeply moved. His love for her grew.

The family became concerned about Jia Baoyu and his undisciplined ways. The casual familiarity of his manner to his own maid, for example, had allowed her to become too friendly, forgetting her place. The family hit on a solution. It was time for him to marry. Lin Daiyu was certainly out of the question; she was always so sickly and morose. The joyful Xue Baochai was certainly more suitable. The matter would have to be handled with some skill, however, because Jia Baoyu would never agree. They would tell him he was going to marry his beloved Lin Daiyu! His bride would come to him hidden under the traditional red wedding veil, and he would never know that it was really Xue Baochai until too late.

Lin Daiyu learned of the marriage but did not know that Jia Baoyu was being tricked. She burned the poems they had written one by one, charged her maid with sending her coffin to await her burial far away from the house, and then died. When Jia Baoyu learned that he had been tricked, he ran to find his darling. But she was already dead. He wept for her and asked himself and heaven where he could go to bring back her soul. Declaring that the house was filled with hatred and that too many had suffered there, he decided to remain in it no longer. Jia Baoyu abandoned the great Jia mansion in disgust for the simple life of a Buddhist monk, renouncing the world and all its evils.

8.5
Jia Baoyu is bored with his studies, envies the freedom of the fish and the birds and thinks of his lovely cousin. Yue opera

Dream of the Red Chamber

8.6 (facing page)
*Jia Baoyu, here played by a woman, and his cousin
Lin Daiyu read the romantic play* The Romance of
the West Chamber. *Huangmei opera*

8.7 (left)
*Jia Baoyu's other cousin is the lively and charming
Xue Baochai. Yue opera*

8.8 (right)
*The melancholic Lin Daiyu collects and buries the
fallen blossoms in the garden, as she sings a
famous aria asking who will bury her after her
death. Yue opera*

8.9
Lin Daiyu and Jia Baoyu declare their love for each other. Huangmei opera

Dream of the Red Chamber

Why Won't You Return?
胡不歸
Cantonese Opera

Why Won't You Return? is a wicked mother-in-law story. The dutiful young wife can do nothing to please the old woman but suffers all patiently out of love for her husband. The story highlights the plight of young women, who were often treated like merchandise by their own families and like servants by their husbands.

Zhao Pinniang was a beautiful young woman who had attracted the unwanted attentions of a wealthy young rake. With an eye on his property, her family employed a matchmaker to formalize an engagement. Zhao Pinniang was resolutely against the bargain and protested. For her defiance, she was expelled from the house and left to fend for herself. With nowhere to go and in great distress, she threw herself in a river to die.

She did not die, however, but was rescued by a childhood friend, Wen Pingsheng. He took her home and resolved to help her. The young man explained the story to his mother and asked for her permission to marry Zhao Pinniang. This was not the kind of match that his mother had hoped for, but she grudgingly agreed. She immediately regretted her acquiescence when no one came to celebrate the wedding. Certainly this must be an unworthy daughter-in-law. Tossed out of her home! Fished out of a river!

After the wedding, Wen Pingsheng had to go off to the military and was only able to return once every ten days. His mother tried to monopolize his time and prevent him from seeing Zhao Pinniang although it was clear that he missed his wife dearly. His affection for his wife made his mother jealous, and she grew harsh to her daughter-in-law. Zhao Pinniang served her dutifully and was rewarded only with scolding. Gradually, her health began to fail, only increasing her mother-in-law's displeasure. This woman had brought nothing but trouble to their house.

Wen Pingsheng returned one day and went straight in to see his wife. He tried to comfort her in her sufferings but was powerless to help. His mother was furious that he had not come to see her first and declared that he had been spoiled by his bad wife. She did not want to see her daughter-in-law any more and moved her out to a garden shed. It was a damp and dirty place that made Zhao Pinniang's illness even more severe.

The army prepared to go to war, and Wen Pingsheng's mother decided that the time had come to break up the marriage. She demanded that her son sign a writ of divorce. Wen Pingsheng begged his mother not to ask this of him, but she pressed him hard. She wailed in front of the ancestral shrine, condemned her son as unfilial, and threatened to smash her own head against the wall if he did not obey her. Finally, and with great sorrow, Wen Pingsheng agreed. But he would write the divorce papers only after he returned. His mother waited for him to leave and went immediately to Zhao Pinniang. She was to collect her baggage and leave immediately. Her husband had agreed to divorce her so she need remain in that house no longer. Zhao Pinniang refused the money that her mother-in-law contemptuously offered and left accompanied by a devoted servant.

8.10
The mother-in-law orders Zhao Pinniang removed to a garden shed at the back of the house. Cantonese opera

Wen Pingsheng returned but could not find his wife. Where had she gone? His mother told him not to trouble himself over that woman any longer. She had another, more promising match already arranged. Wen Pingsheng ran out in distress to find his beloved wife but found instead her servant. The servant told him that her sufferings had finally been too much for Zhao Pinniang. She was already dead. He followed the servant to his wife's grave and cried out for her to return to him.

But Zhao Pinniang was still alive. Her tomb was only a device to free him from any attachment to her. When she saw the depth of his love for her she could not help but reveal herself, and the couple was reunited. Even the hard heart of Wen Pingsheng's mother softened at their reunion. The family was reconciled.

8.11
Wen Pingsheng prepares to leave his beloved wife and go to war. Cantonese opera

The Purple Hairpin
紫釵記
Cantonese Opera

Tang Xianzu was a dramatic genius and a contemporary of Shakespeare. He wrote five memorable plays. Each was very long, running to over fifty scenes. They stand among the highest literary achievements in China, blending poetry, prose, argument, music, and dance in *kunqu* dramatic style. One is *The Purple Hairpin*, which is based on a piece of Tang dynasty literature, *The Story of Huo Xiaoyu*. Cantonese opera dramatist Tang Disheng reworked the fifty-three scenes of Tang Xianzu's play into a shorter, nine-act piece in the 1950s. In this work, unlike the original, the audience discovers what happens to the wicked Commander Lu and the identity of the mysterious man in yellow.

A young gentleman, Li Yi, went out with his cousin and a friend to enjoy a display of lanterns after the New Year Festival. While admiring the lanterns, he saw a beautiful young woman frantically searching for something. Li Yi found a lovely purple ornamental hairpin on the ground and guessed that the lady must have lost this treasure. Speaking to her maid, he discovered that the beauty was Xiaoyu of the house of Huo. Huo Xiaoyu was frantic because she had lost a very valuable hairpin fashioned by a master craftsman. Li Yi went over and spoke to her. He was completely smitten and resolved to marry her. The next day he approached a matchmaker and presented her with the pin to return to the Huo family along with his offer of marriage. Huo Xiaoyu had been favourably impressed with the young man and so the family agreed.

After their marriage, Li Yi declared that it was time for him to take the official exams in the capital. His new wife was worried that he would not return and might be tempted or pressed into marrying another. Li Yi comforted her and wrote out a pledge of his love and loyalty. He went to the capital and did very well. But that is when his troubles began. He neglected to go to his home town and pay his respects to Commander Lu, who was in charge of the district. Commander Lu was already displeased with Li Yi because earlier the young man had had the effrontery to reject the great opportunity of marrying his daughter. So the commander assigned the new graduate to a post far away at the frontier, keeping Li Yi and his wife separated for three long years.

Huo Xiaoyu, left alone to support herself, began selling off her jewellery. She despaired of seeing her husband again, and her health began to decline. Finally, she sent her servant to sell the precious purple hairpin. The hairpin eventually made its way into the hands of Commander Lu, who recognized it and found use for it. He had recently brought Li Yi back from the frontier, where the young man had distinguished himself. The commander appointed him as his own adjutant and pressured him to marry his daughter. Li Yi's own wife, he argued, had given him up long ago to marry someone else. Look, he declared, she had even sold the token of their marriage, the purple hairpin. When Li Yi saw the hairpin, he caved in and agreed to the marriage.

8.12
Li Yi and Huo Xiaoyu say their farewells while the official escort awaits. Cantonese opera

The Purple Hairpin

Li Yi's cousin and friend discovered the truth and told it all to Huo Xiaoyu. They lamented over the tragedy and denounced the trickery of the commander, but what could they do? It was then that a mysterious benefactor appeared. His name, he said, was 'the man in yellow.' He had overheard their troubles and would help, providing all that was necessary for a great reunion feast for Li Yi and Huo Xiaoyu. Later he would do something further. Li Yi accepted an invitation to a special banquet but found himself led to Huo Xiaoyu. There, 'the man in yellow' reunited the couple in happiness, then left the banquet hall to deal with Commander Lu.

The mysterious stranger was in reality a close relative of the emperor and often went about in disguise to learn about the people. He revealed his true identify, accused the commander of misusing his authority, and mustered evidence of other wrongdoings. The commander was found guilty and executed for his crimes.

8.13 (facing page)
Huo Xiaoyu puts on her finery for the lantern festival. Cantonese opera

8.14
The mysterious 'man in yellow' overhears Huo Xiaoyu's complaints in a Buddhist temple. Cantonese opera

Pi Jin Plays the Fool
皮金滾燈
Sichuan Opera

Many plays in the Chinese opera are show-pieces for the physical or vocal abilities of the performer. The play sets up a situation in which a performer can show off a particular skill to the limit. *Pi Jin Plays the Fool* is a vehicle for the clown role performer to show what he can really do. In addition to its wonderful acrobatics, this play shows that the clown role in Chinese theatre is not limited to commoners. A rich man can be a clown, as can a general or even a high official. Class or position cannot disguise clownishness for very long.

Pi Jin was the son of a very wealthy man. He married a woman from a good family, also with money and influence. His new wife quickly discovered that her husband was a fool, an idler, and a wastrel. She had to do something. Her solution was to put him through a series of impossible moves and positions while balancing a lit lamp on his head. Thus chastened, he would resolve to live a better life or be put through such torture again.

8.15 (facing page)
Pi Jin's formidable wife decides that the time has come to take him in hand. Sichuan opera

8.16
The clown performs one of a number of bizarre acrobatic positions at his wife's bidding. Sichuan opera

The Romance of the West Chamber
西廂記
Yue Opera

The Romance of the West Chamber is one of China's favourite love stories. It is also one of China's oldest. Like *The Story of Huo Xiaoyu*, on which *The Purple Hairpin* is based, *The Romance of the West Chamber* comes from a short tale of the Tang dynasty. In this play, the entire action takes place in a single location, a Buddhist monastery. It was, and indeed still is, common practice for people in search of quiet to stay at a Buddhist temple. Scholars prepared for exams there, and travellers sought rest under the care of the monks. *The Romance of the West Chamber* is a story of love at first sight, a broken promise, and stratagems to overcome family opposition.

A young gentleman named Zhang Junrui stopped at a temple on his way to the capital. While there, he caught sight of another visitor, a beautiful woman, and instantly fell in love. He learned from one of the monks that she was the daughter of a great family. Her name was Cui Yingying, and she had come to the temple with her mother and maid to mourn the death of her father. Every evening, Cui Yingying and her servant burned incense in the garden in his memory. That night, Zhang Junrui hid himself among the bushes so that he could observe her. As the monk had said, Cui Yingying came out at the appointed time and burnt incense. She discovered her secret admirer in hiding and asked him who he was and what business he had there. Zhang Junrui introduced himself and the two immediately fell in love as if destined for each other.

But Zhang Junrui was not Cui Yingying's only admirer. A bandit chief, Flying Tiger, also learned that the beautiful daughter of a great house was staying at the temple. He surrounded it with his men and demanded that

Cui Yingying be given over to him. Her mother panicked. She offered her daughter's hand to anyone who could save them from this calamity. This offer was the perfect opportunity for Zhang Junrui. He wrote a letter to a general who happened to be a good friend of his and entrusted it to a monk who excelled in the martial arts. The letter got through, the general came, and the bandits fled.

Zhang Junrui was delighted and impatient to claim his prize, the Lady Cui Yingying. Her mother invited him to their quarters to toast their good fortune. They raised their glasses and just as they were about to drink, the older woman announced that now they could consider themselves siblings. Both were dumbfounded. They had expected to become wife and husband, not sister and brother! But Cui Yingying's mother had had time to reconsider her rash promise, and she was not going to arrange a marriage for her daughter with just anybody.

Zhang Junrui became heartsick and an invalid in the temple's west chamber. As he could not visit Cui Yingying, her maid, Hongniang, became a go-between. She carried love letters back and forth, and one night brought her mistress to him. The maid then found herself shut out of the west chamber by the lovers. Cui Yingying's mother, suspicious that her daughter was still carrying on a liaison with the young gentleman, forced the maid to tell her everything. She summoned her daughter and Zhang Junrui and told him that if he ever expected to marry Cui Yingying he must go away and distinguish himself in the exams and obtain a high official position. Only that would be good enough for the family. Finally, Zhang Junrui accepted the conditions, said his farewells and left for the capital.

8.17
After the maid has acted as go-between, the two young lovers meet in the west chamber. Yue opera

8.18 (facing page)
Strolling about the temple, Zhang Junrui praises Cui Yingying's elegance and beauty. Yue opera

8.19 (facing page)
Cui Yingying is impressed with the handsome
young scholar. Yue opera

8.20
The lovers are disconsolate on learning that they
must consider themselves brother and sister rather
than husband and wife. Zhang Junrui pins his
hopes for approval on winning honours in the
national examination. Yue opera

WEALTHY FAMILIES

Chapter 9

Common Folk:
Those Who Are Ruled

THE PHILOSOPHER MENCIUS wrote in the third century BC, before the rise of a mercantile class, about two broad social groups: the rulers and the ruled. The rulers are the educated, the scholar class; the ruled are all those socially below it. A traditional classification system of Chinese society arranges all people below the rank of emperor into four basic groups: scholar-officials, peasants, artisans, and merchants. The last three make up the ruled. It is interesting that the peasant class is second only to the Confucian literati in this reckoning, a placement that acknowledges peasants as the prime producers for the nation. Artisans fashion what is produced, and merchants, at the bottom of the scale, simply market it. Throughout history peasants have constituted 80 per cent of the Chinese population. The importance of their agricultural work was honoured in imperial ritual. The emperor turned the soil in ritual ploughing and was responsible for offering sacrifices to ensure that heaven would bless the country with abundant harvests.

Despite this recognition, peasants have had hard lives, struggling with the land usually for little more than subsistence. The state could intervene in the lives of common folk in several ways: requiring men to work on unpaid forced labour projects; pressing them into military service; and levying taxes for special projects. Peasants, pressed into debt because of state obligations, droughts, floods, or poor harvests, often became further constrained as tenant farmers. Typically, half the harvest went to the landowner.

The dream of social mobility, primarily through study, was in effect closed to peasants and their children because of poverty. Children, in fact, could be sold or traded to settle debts or bring some much-needed cash into the family. Justice could prove elusive if peasants did not have the resources to bribe local magistrates, who depended on 'red envelopes' to supplement the meagre state stipend. Peasant women, and in particular widows, were especially vulnerable.

The poor on the Chinese stage wear simple costumes with large, coloured patches. Common men often, though not always, appear in clown make-up, a white patch painted around the nose and eyes. The patch indicates lowness, such as that in a small-minded lackey or a clownish servant. Plays with common people run the range from tragic to comic.

9.1
Madam Jiao and Cao Zhuang, in Slay the Dog. *Qin opera*

The Jade Bracelet
拾玉鐲
Ping and Cantonese Opera

The Jade Bracelet is a popular piece performed in several regional opera styles. Peking, Cantonese, Anhui, Yue, and Hebei Clapper opera all include it in their repertoire. It is also one of those operas that regularly make their way into the programs of companies touring outside of China. The reason is simple. The play is a straightforward story that depends primarily on mime and thus is accessible for most audiences. It has comic characterizations and charming double entendre. Much of its delight comes from Mother Liu, a female clown usually played by a man. Her loose jacket, long pipe, and characteristic walk bring smiles to audiences both in and out of China. The high point of her performance is imitating a young woman coyly picking up a young man's gift.

One fine day a young village maiden, Sun Yujiao, found herself alone. Her mother had gone to the local Buddhist temple. Sun Yujiao fed the chickens and then decided to do a daring thing for a Chinese maiden. She sat alone outside the door embroidering a handkerchief. Fu Peng, a handsome scholar, happened by and while chasing the chickens out of his way with his fan came face to face with the maiden. She was so startled and attracted by the young man that she pricked herself with her needle. He, in turn, was struck by her loveliness. Sun Yujiao hurriedly explained that her mother was not at home and went inside, barring the gate as a modest young girl should. Meanwhile, the local busybody, Mother Liu, turned up. She saw the young scholar leave a jade bracelet on the ground declaring that if the maiden picked it up she would end up as his wife. Mother Liu crept over to look at the bracelet and then with a laugh decided to conceal herself to watch what would happen.

Sun Yujiao came out again and discovered the bracelet. She wanted it, but what if she were seen? She pretended to call out for her mother, all the while deftly kicking the bracelet closer to the house. Finally, she dropped her handkerchief over top of the bracelet and then scooped them both up, thus preserving her modesty. Fu Peng, however, saw that she had the bracelet. She was overcome with embarrassment, but he left satisfied that she had taken up his gift.

Mother Liu watched Sun Yujiao go back in and decided that now was the time to have a little fun. She knocked at the door saying that she had come for a visit. The arrival of the

notorious gossip threw Sun Yujiao into a panic. She tried to hide the bracelet but nowhere seemed safe. Finally, she pushed it up her right arm under her sleeve. Mother Liu entered the house and was determined to catch the young girl out. She cried out in alarm that a big bug had settled on the girl's head. Sun Yujiao acted too fast. Reaching out for the bug, she exposed her wrist and the precious jade bracelet.

Sun Yujiao tried to make up stories to explain how she came by such a thing, but Mother Liu just laughed. Getting up, she pantomimed the whole affair from kicking the bracelet to 'accidentally' dropping the handkerchief. Sun Yujiao went on her knees in embarrassment and distress. Having had her joke, Mother Liu now revealed that she had really wanted to help all along. She offered to take Sun Yujiao's handkerchief as a gift to the young scholar in return for the bracelet. That exchange would seal their intentions to marry. The young girl was so excited. How long before it would be accomplished? Mother Liu said she needed only a little patience – three years should do it.

'Three years!' cried out Sun Yujiao in alarm. But it was just another of Mother Liu's jokes. She assured the young girl that everything would be settled in just three days.

9.2
Sun Yujiao is delighted with the gift of the jade bracelet. She wears an apron indicating she is a peasant girl and a headdress common to young women on the operatic stage. Ping opera

9.3
Sun Yujiao slips the bracelet on her wrist thinking she can hide it from the nosy neighbour, Mother Liu. Cantonese opera

9.4
Mother Liu, in her loose jacket and holding her pipe, has finished teasing. When can Mother Liu arrange the match? Why, in three days! Ping opera

The Jade Bracelet

Liu Ling Gets Drunk
劉伶醉酒
Ping Opera

Marco Polo reported that the inhabitants of Cathay drank an excellent wine made of rice with an assortment of spices. He praised it as better than any other wine: beautifully clear and speedily intoxicating. The Chinese are very proud of their strong drink, and it often figures prominently in stories of sages, immortals or, as in this case, a commoner about to become immortal through his love of and ability to hold his wine.

Liu Ling was a famous drinker. He could outdrink anyone in the tavern and was proud of this natural talent. One day, he went into the village and to his surprise saw that a brand new wine shop had opened up. A sign outside the shop boasted that the owner would supply three years of free liquor to anyone who did not get drunk on his wine. Liu Ling was amazed and felt that he had to take up the challenge. He would show this upstart of a shopkeeper. First he would drink him dry and then he would smash his sign for him.

But the shopkeeper was none other than Du Kang, the wine immortal. Du Kang politely invited Liu Ling in and asked him to choose his wine. Liu Ling, knowledgeable about such things, chose the very best wine in the shop. He drank his first cup, but nothing happened. He drank his second cup, but still nothing happened. Du Kang prepared yet another cup for this formidable customer, but this time slipped something into the wine. After Liu Ling drank it down he began to feel dizzy. It was incredible, but he felt flushed. Liu Ling turned around to speak to the shopkeeper, but Du Kang had vanished into the air. He now understood who this mysterious shopkeeper was. What's more, he reasoned, there could only be one reason for this apparition. Du Kang had come to take one

of his own: Liu Ling was about to become a wine immortal, too.

Liu Ling quickly went home and told his wife the whole story. He did not know what was in the wine, but he would surely die soon and then join the immortals. His wife was very pleased. After all, she could then go around saying that she was the wife of a heavenly immortal. Liu Ling gave her last-minute instructions. The Chinese custom was to burn paper money for the dead to use on their journey to the other life. But she should not bother with that. Instead, she was to hang up a placard outside the house and invite all his friends to come and drink in celebration. Neither should she put out the usual offerings of fruit to his spirit. Three big barrels of wine would do nicely. His wife was puzzled. Why three big barrels of wine? How silly of her! The first was to get him into the nether world, the second was to bribe the keeper of the ghost gate, and the third was for him to play drinking games with the king of the dead. And she need not bother with a coffin at all. All she needed to do was stuff his body in a wine cask and pickle him. That way he would be able to smell the sweet aroma of wine forever in the other world.

9.5
Liu Ling begins to feel the wine go to his head.
Ping opera

Liu Ling Gets Drunk

9.6 *(facing page)*
The wine has taken its full effect. Ping opera

9.7
The wine immortal, Du Kang, supports the tipsy
Liu Ling. Ping opera

A Gift of Wine

王茂生進酒

Chaozhou Opera

The charming story of Wang Maosheng and his wine has the quality of a parable. A simple gift from a simple man is transformed into something precious through a friend's gratitude. Doorkeepers, meant to keep people apart, are turned into instruments of welcome and reunion. The play ends with a toast to the virtues of friendship and generosity.

Wang Maosheng and his wife were poor peasants. A severe drought had forced them to abandon their home in search of work and food. They begged, but without much success. They were just at their wits' end when they learned that the emperor had installed a new prince, Xue Rengui, for winning a great victory on the battlefield. Wang Maosheng's hopes soared. He had known the prince many years ago, when Xue Rengui had been a poor wanderer with no place to go. Wang Maosheng and his wife had taken him in and given him whatever meagre food they had. Surely he would remember their kindness and help them now that they were in such difficulty. But everyone was going to the new prince with congratulatory gifts. What could they bring? Wang Maosheng had a talent for making wine, but he had neither jug nor ingredients. All he and his wife had left were an old vegetable jar and a single piece of red paper. Well, that was what they would give. They filled the jar with water and fixed the red paper to it as a label marked 'wine.'

The couple arrived at the home of the new prince full of expectation. The doorkeeper took one look at the beggars and was determined to keep them out. He took their jar and letter of introduction and told them to go away. Xue Rengui discovered their letter and scolded the doorkeeper for driving away these good people. They were to be brought to him at once! The

9.8 (facing page)
The officious doorkeeper won't let just anyone in to see the new prince. Chaozhou opera

9.9
At the direction of the new prince, the doorkeeper helps Wang Maosheng into proper clothes, but the poor man just cannot get used to them. Chaozhou opera

nervous doorkeeper searched until he found them and prepared them to meet the new prince. First, they had to be suitably dressed; their beggars' rags would not do. Wang Maosheng would have preferred those rags; he just could not get used to the fine robes. Finally, the doorkeeper presented them to the prince, who received them with all respect and honours. The prince promised to punish the doorkeeper and bring his good friends to live in the mansion with him. Wang Maosheng pleaded for clemency for the doorkeeper, who after all was only doing his job. As for the moving in, well, he was used to life on a farm, not in a great house.

The prince smiled at Wang Maosheng's simplicity. He would drink a cup of Wang Maosheng's own wine in tribute. What good wine it was, the best ever given to him! Wang Maosheng was amazed. It was just plain water. There was nothing to it at all. But Wang Maosheng's water was indeed the best wine, for it was a pledge that their friendship would never die. The prince invited his junior officials to drink this excellent 'wine' too. At first a look of bewilderment crossed their faces, but then all declared that this was certainly good wine. Xue Rengui then picked up the whole jar and drank it down in honour of his friend.

9.10
Prince Xue Rengui, wearing his official's hat and belt, drinks deeply from Wang Maosheng's jar of water. It is the best 'wine' he has ever tasted. Chaozhou opera

A Gift of Wine

The Story of Dou E
實娥冤
Jiangxi Opera

Dou E's story is one of abuse, murder, and injustice. It has had a long history. The master dramatist, Guan Hanqing, wrote it as a four-act play in the thirteenth century, a time when the Chinese keenly felt discrimination and injustice at the hands of their Mongol conquerors. A sixteenth-century dramatist wrote *Tale of the Golden Lock,* basing it on Guan Hanqing's work and even incorporating the third act of the original. Since then, various regional operas have retold the story under titles like *The Unjust Case of Dou E That Moved Heaven and Earth* and *June Snow.* Commoners could easily relate to a play in which the innocent and defenceless suffer at the hands of corruption. They knew too well how hard justice was to come by without influence. Justice does prevail in the story, but it takes a miracle and is too late to save Dou E.

Dou Tianzhang was a destitute scholar who owed money to the widow Cai but could not possibly repay it. He wanted desperately to go to the capital to try his hand at the exams and improve the family's fortunes, yet he could not afford to go. He decided to give his daughter, Dou E, to the widow to cancel the debt. His daughter would serve her and eventually marry her son. The arrangements were made, and so Dou E dutifully left her father to fulfil the bargain. Dou E was a model of Confucian filiality and served the widow well. She did indeed marry but soon became a widow herself. Thus, Dou E was left to mourn her husband and take care of her aged mother-in-law.

Such a filial and beautiful young widow could only attract attention. A local bully, Donkey Zhang, was set on marrying the pretty daughter-in-law. Dou E was horrified and resisted. In order to force her into the marriage,

Donkey Zhang schemed to poison the widow Cai, thus leaving Dou E alone, but the plan went wrong and Donkey Zhang's own father ate the poison in a soup, promptly dying. The bully accused Dou E of murder, and as she was still unwilling to marry him took her to court. The court was a travesty, with a corrupt and easily bribed magistrate. Paid off, the magistrate ordered Dou E flogged until she confessed. When she did not, he ordered the widow Cai flogged in front of her daughter-in-law. Dou E could not bear to see the old woman suffer so and confessed to the murder. The confession sealed her fate.

On the day of execution, Dou E faced her accusers and called on heaven to demonstrate her innocence. She asked for a long white silk streamer to be attached to a flagpole before her death and predicted that her blood would flow up into the strip of silk without staining the ground. It would snow in June to cover her corpse, and then a terrible drought would descend on the land for three long years. Dou E was executed, and all that she predicted came to pass.

9.11
Dou E, tied to a stake and guarded, has confessed to a crime she did not commit to save the widow Cai, who lies weeping at her feet. Jiangxi opera

The Story of Dou E

Years later, Dou E's father finally returned. He had been successful in the exams and promoted to the rank of inspector general, with responsibility to tour the districts and examine the affairs of local magistrates. Now back home, he looked through the local records late into the night and fell asleep. Dou E's ghost appeared and cried out the whole tragic story, demanding justice. Inspector Dou awoke and, convinced that the vision was true, summoned all concerned to court. It soon became clear that Donkey Zhang had bought the poison and that he was the real murderer. The truth was revealed and punishment meted out. The inspector general ordered the bully executed and the magistrate stripped of office. Justice was satisfied, but too late for Dou E.

9.12 (facing page)
The executioners carry Dou E off to her fate while the sky promises disaster for this injustice. Jiangxi opera

9.13
The ghost of Dou E appears to her father in a dream. He must right this terrible wrong. Jiangxi opera

'Dream of the Coronet and the Belt'
夜夢冠帶
Jiangxi Opera

'Dream of the Coronet and Belt' is a short scene from the play *Water before the Horse.* Like many other plays on the Chinese stage, this one holds out the possibility of social mobility. But social mobility can work down as well as up. Just as the audience can enjoy a model of success, it also can have the satisfaction of seeing foolish pride get what it deserves.

Cui could not stand her poverty any longer. She was married to a poor scholar who did not seem to hold out any promise for the future. Cui yearned for fine things, but how was she going to get them as a poor scholar's wife? She nagged her husband into writing out a certificate of divorce. The ex-wife would use her new freedom to make some changes. She soon married again and this time found a better match. Cui was more comfortable than she had ever been but this, too, was not enough.

One night a wonderful thing happened. An imperial messenger came, announcing that the emperor himself had honoured her house. He sent to her an imperial belt and coronet as signs of his favour. Cui was beside herself with joy.

9.14 (facing page)
Cui has a wonderful dream. Attended by numerous servant girls, she is giddy with joy at her good fortune. Jiangxi opera

9.15 (above)
Cui flaunts her good fortune, not knowing she is about to wake up to reality. Jiangxi opera

9.16 (right)
Cui dreams she is attended by four maids while a messenger from the palace stands behind to give her an imperial headdress. Cui holds the belt with pride, already cultivating a studied arrogance. Jiangxi opera

It was too good to be true! This honour meant status and undoubtedly riches. She revelled in her new-found power and abused the messenger as she exercised a delicious arrogance. But it *was* too good to be true. She suddenly woke to find that it had all been a dream.

Later in *Water before the Horse* Cui is reduced to poverty again after running through her new husband's money. This time her position is worse than before and she is now forced to beg. She is shocked to learn that her first husband has finally been recognized and appointed to an official rank. Ashamed as she is, Cui plans to beg him to take her back. The new official, mounted on a fine horse, tells a servant to scatter water on the ground in front of him. Could she gather up the spilled water? If she could get back spilled water, declares her husband, he would take her back, too. Cui can only look on in helpless dismay.

Third Wife Teaches Her Son
三娘教子
Jin Opera

Third Wife is another model of Confucian virtue. She sacrifices herself to hard work and poverty to uphold the memory of her husband. The Chinese theatre has many such models. Wives were expected to endure years of hardship while husbands left to take exams in the capital or conduct affairs. The proper wife remained patient during this absence and was attentive to her husband's parents and children. The first wife had the highest position in a household; a third wife was relatively insignificant. Yet this story demonstrates that it is not status but behaviour that makes a person praiseworthy.

A merchant said farewell to his three wives and set off by ship on a business trip. That was the last anyone saw of him. News came back that the ship had been wrecked in a storm and there were no survivors. The first wife, knowing that she had to look out for herself, took her share of the family fortune and married again. The second wife followed suit and left behind the merchant's little son. The third wife, Wang Chun'e, however, pledged to keep her husband's memory alive. She would care for the boy as her own son with the help of an old, faithful servant.

But the little money remaining quickly ran out, and Wang Chun'e found herself in dreadful poverty. She worked day and night at a loom, weaving cloth to earn a little money to keep the boy in school. Perhaps one day he would take the exams and win honours for the family name. Her hopes were soon disappointed. The boy was unwilling to study and came home early one day to announce that he was not going back. The other children had teased him for not having a real mother. Wang Chun'e told him to memorize his lessons, but when she tested him she found he had learned nothing at all. It was only the intercession of the old servant that prevented her from striking the boy for his stupidity and ingratitude. But Wang Chun'e would teach him a lesson he would never forget. She walked to her loom and slashed to shreds the cloth she had been labouring over, declaring she would no longer work for this foolish son.

The boy was deeply moved and begged for forgiveness. He returned to school and worked so hard that he eventually won top honours in the capital. Returning home to tell Wang Chun'e the happy news, he found an even greater surprise awaiting him. His father had survived the shipwreck and prospered as an official. Now, he had returned home. Third Wife finally saw the fruits of her loyalty and hard work in the reunited family.

9.17
Finding that the son has not learned his lessons, Wang Chun'e threatens to beat him. Jin opera

9.18 (facing page)
The tearful boy, in this case played by a young woman, listens to Wang Chun'e as she cries out her famous aria. Her scolding teaches him an important lesson. Jin opera

Chapter 10   The Religious

THREE MAJOR IDEOLOGIES have contended for prominence in China: Confucianism, Taoism, and Buddhism. Over time the three have overlapped in popular understanding and practice, and people now see them as complementary rather than contradictory. It is not unusual to see Buddhist saints, Taoist gods, and Confucian classics all in the same house.

Confucianism is an ethical system, not a religion at all, yet it has its temples and honours its sages. Its precepts, which have infused society from the fourth century BC, clearly outline everyone's place and responsibility. Confucianism became the organizing principle for all of Chinese society as well as the measure of scholarly ability. Taoism emphasizes quietism and unity with the way of the universe. It teaches that the universe is animated by an energy called *qi* and that all things have their place in a balance of two opposing forces: *yin* and *yang.* Through the centuries, Taoism has incorporated many elements of folk religion and alchemy, acquiring a vast pantheon of gods and immortals. Taoist priests studied nature, communed with the gods, and exorcised demons. Buddhism came to China from India and developed in unique ways under the genius of Chinese religious innovators. It has enjoyed great support but also suffered severe persecution. Many points in its doctrine were incompatible with the Chinese world view. The concept of monks and nuns who had cut themselves off from their families was totally antithetical to the long tradition of family unity. The Buddhist rejection of the world as illusory and a place of suffering contrasted with the positive view of the Taoists and the worldliness of the Confucians. Finally, Buddhism was a foreign doctrine competing with indigenous Confucianism and Taoism for influence among people and in high places.

People who have committed themselves to the religious life form a distinct group in Chinese social structure. They have turned their backs on the world, left their families, cut their hair as a symbol of austerity, and taken new names. The Chinese stage has its religious characters, but they are not one-dimensional. Many stage religious reveal that their hearts are not really in their vocation; they are monks or nuns only because they are running away from injustice or oppression. Although dressed in habits they act in a very worldly manner, delighting the audience with comic antics. Others are clearly villains. Fahai, the Buddhist monk in *The Legend of the White Snake*, is a busybody and an enemy of true love. The old

10.1
The monk Fahai, in The Legend of the White Snake. *Sichuan opera*

mother superior in *The Emperor's Daughter* is prepared to sell the princess-turned-nun for blood money.

The plays in this section emphasize the human side of those in the religious life. One Buddhist monk cannot suppress his old cravings for meat and drink. A young monk and nun yearn for life and love in the world. Another nun suffers a mother's agony for the son she dare not acknowledge. These characters are not distant or severe; they are presented as people with hopes and failings like the rest of humanity.

The Thirsty Monk

醉打山門

Peking Opera

Many monks in China were renowned for their martial arts skills. Physical training provided a balance for the extended periods of quiet meditation. Thus the arts of *taiji* (often written *tai chi*) and *gongfu* (or *kung fu*) developed in the temples along religious, cosmic principles. Lu Zhishen, in *The Thirsty Monk*, was an accomplished fighter before he became a religious. The play gives him an opportunity to practise these skills before the audience and show his human, indeed comic, side.

The monk Lu Zhishen went for a walk down the Five-Terraced Mountain to shake off his melancholy. He had entered religious life a year ago but somehow was not getting the hang of it. Yes, he had cut his hair and entered a community but still could not learn the sutras chanted in the temple. As for fasting, well, his strong suit had always been eating meat and drinking wine. A meagre bowl of vegetables and plain water just did not seem fit for a hearty eater like Lu Zhishen. He was not much of a peacemaker either. If he saw something he did not like, he could hardly refrain from getting up and killing someone.

Actually, it was this impetuousness and outrage against injustice that had landed him in a Buddhist temple in the first place. He was once a captain in a military court. Everyone had feared him for his imposing size and unmanageable temper. His life had changed when he killed a local bully for cheating and forcing his attentions on a young, destitute girl. Now a wanted murderer, the captain had fled from the law and hidden himself away as a monk.

It had become clear that the religious life was too difficult for a man of his habits and temper. Lu Zhishen hoped that a change of scenery would make him feel better and so

started out on a walk. Who should come across his path, however, but an itinerant wine seller singing his country song. This temptation was just too much. Lu Zhishen greeted the wine seller and suggested that he rest a bit. He must be exhausted from carrying such a heavy load of wine! Why was he carrying two buckets of wine up the mountain anyway? Was it for the monks there? The wine seller laughed at such an idea. He would sell his wine but not to monks. The abbot would have something to say about that if he did!

'The two of us were destined to meet,' Lu Zhishen said eagerly. Catching on to this peculiar monk's craving for wine, the wine seller retorted, 'You and the king of hell are destined to meet!' and he attempted to go on his way. 'Stop!' shouted the monk. 'Put that wine down!' When the wine seller refused, Lu Zhishen grabbed him with powerful hands and forced him to the ground. The poor vendor struggled as best he could but was no match for the monk.

He reminded Lu Zhishen that monks had chosen the spiritual life. Yes, yes, Lu Zhishen knew all about that, but a life with no meat or strong drink was such a bore. Wine was just better than water or tea for quenching a big man's thirst. Suddenly, Lu Zhishen pointed down the path. 'Look, the abbot is coming!' The wine seller quickly turned to see. The monk even more quickly scooped up the wine buckets and drank them down one after the other, spinning about as he drained the last drops in each.

The wine seller, furious at the trick, demanded payment. But now Lu Zhishen became quite the holy monk and prayerfully claimed special status as a religious, chanting the mantra 'O Mi Tuo Fo.' The vendor insisted and finally

10.2 (facing page)
The wine seller refuses to stay and chat, but Lu Zhishen forces him to put his buckets of wine down. Peking opera

10.3
The thirsty monk twists the arm of the wine seller for a drink. Peking opera

the monk gave him his rosary beads, bragging that he actually could drink an ocean of wine. That little bit in two buckets was nothing. The wine seller called him out on that outrageous boast. 'Open your mouth and if all that wine is really gone I won't charge you.' Lu Zhishen opened wide to prove what a great drinker he was. The wine seller peeked in, stuffed it with the rosary beads, and ran off. The monk, now left alone and feeling the wine, decided to practise his legendary fighting skills by a little roadside pavilion. His exercises caused the whole place to shake and echo with peals of thunder. Having worked off his melancholy, Lu Zhishen returned to the temple to sleep off the wine.

10.4
The monk downs a bucket of wine while deftly kicking the protesting wine seller out of his way. Peking opera

The Thirsty Monk

Two Flee Religious Life
雙下山
Anhui and Yue Opera

The common term for religious is *chujiaren*, or 'those who have left their families.' As the concept of family has always been very strong in China, leaving is a serious matter. It means severing relationships and attachments. It also means a new name. In this story, the monk Benwu's name means 'emptiness,' and the nun Wuming's name means 'clear awareness.' Both these names express Buddhist doctrines for the religious life. The goals of those who bear the names, however, are quite different.

Benwu had had enough. He had been a Buddhist monk for many years but could no longer stand the rigours of religious life and the strictness of his master. It was not as if he had chosen this life for himself. Not at all! In fact, his parents had sent him to the monastery as a child after listening to a bogus fortune teller. Well, he was no longer a child, and the time had come to get himself out of this situation.

Benwu seized a chance to slip away from the temple and hurried his way down the mountain. He did not know where he was going exactly, but at least he was free from the discipline of a life that was not for him. As he descended the mountain, Benwu came across someone unexpected, a Buddhist nun. Who was she and what was she doing here away from her community?

She said that her name was Wuming and that she was from the Fairy Peach Convent, on her way to visit her parents. Benwu knew that her actions were unusual; as a religious she had 'gone forth from the family' and should have no such attachments. As the two chatted, they became increasingly reluctant to part company. Finally, however, they exchanged their courtesies and set off on their ways.

Wuming thought about the charming young monk as she followed the mountain path. He seemed to be in such a rush that he surely must be running away. Benwu thought about the pretty nun. That story about visiting her parents could not possibly be true. She must be running away, too. How could he find out for sure? His chance was soon to come. An abandoned temple stood on the side of the path he was taking down the mountain. He looked inside and discovered that Wuming was there, apparently asleep. All he had to do was to imitate the voice of a scolding old mother superior and watch Wuming's reaction. That should make everything clear. Wuming, who was only

pretending to sleep, did not give him the chance. She cried out in alarm, pointing to an old abbot out of the window. Benwu jumped in consternation but then realized he had been tricked.

He admitted to Wuming that he was indeed running away and told her his story. Wuming confessed that she, too, had slipped away. She had never wanted to be a religious either. Her parents had sold her as a concubine to a rich man during a great famine, but she did not want to go. She had run away to the only place she could think of, a convent. Now, like him, she yearned to return to the world. The two quickly realized how much they had in common. Surely meeting like this demonstrated that they were destined for each other. They resolved to continue their journey to a new life, but now together.

10.5
Wuming, dressed in a theatrical nun's habit embroidered with the character for Buddha, has left her convent for the worldly life. Anhui opera

10.6
The monk and the nun, back to back, are not sure what to make of each other when they first meet. Anhui opera

10.7 *(facing page)*
Wuming and Benwu continue down the mountain to seek their happiness together. Yue opera

Two Flee Religious Life

Finding Mother in a Convent

游庵認母
Yue Opera

Several Chinese operas deal with the conflict between advancing up the social scale and recognizing humble beginnings. Sometimes their birth is an embarrassment to ambitious officials. They look for ways to deny their parents or wives to avoid spoiling their careers. Such officials are clearly condemned on the stage. Xu Yuanzai, in *Finding Mother in a Convent*, is not of that kind. He is determined to pursue the truth no matter where it leads.

Xu Yuanzai was an accomplished scholar, a degree holder with a bright future. His past, however, was clouded. His name was not really Xu. The Xu family had adopted Yuanzai as a baby after he had been abandoned. Who had abandoned him? Why had they done so? Was it because of poverty? Were they criminals wanted by the state? Xu Yuanzai grew up believing that there was no thread left to lead him back to his first parents.

On the verge of a great career as an official, he discovered an old letter penned in blood, hidden away in a trunk. Xu Yuanzai read the letter and realized that it had been written by his mother and hidden in his baby blanket before she abandoned him. He trembled with excitement. Here were riddles that would reveal the names of his first parents, and now that he was a scholar he would be able to solve them easily.

The riddles led Xu Yuanzai to the Fahua Convent. There he discovered a nun, Zhizhen, whose name meant 'firm in truth.' Could this nun be his mother? If she was, she was not admitting to anything. Zhizhen was, however, in a great panic. She recognized the young scholar as her own son come to find her out. She had had a love affair in her youth but being a nun could not possibly raise a child. So

she had written a letter begging that a kind-hearted family would take in her baby. She was determined not to reveal her secret now. She was afraid for her son if the truth of his birth came out. He was about to enter a promising career, and her identity might hinder or even ruin him. She was also afraid for herself because to recognize her son meant admitting that she had broken the discipline of her vows.

Xu Yuanzai tried double entendre. Seeing pine cones on the ground, he asked Zhizhen how the mother tree could not be concerned

about losing her children. Zhizhen replied that it was not that the mother tree did not care but only that the wind and the rains had bent it until the tree no longer had any strength. Xu Yuanzai tried again. He asked her about the many bamboo shoots he saw. Did the nun think that the bamboo did not care for its own shoots? Zhizhen answered that it was not that the bamboo did not care but only that its roots did not go deep and could not withstand the gnawing of so many insects. How could it defend itself?

Nothing Xu Yuanzai said or did brought him closer to the truth until he discovered a portrait in Zhizhen's cell of a man who looked almost like him. The nun could stand it no longer and admitted that she was indeed his mother. The two had a tearful reunion and embraced as mother and son for the first time.

10.8
Zhizhen, her graceful water sleeves extended and the characteristic tasselled whisk of a Buddhist in evidence, is in anguish over the visit of her son. Yue opera

10.9 (facing page)
The nun Zhizhen tries to put off the persistent scholar seeking his past. Yue opera

Chapter 11   Outlaws

OUTLAWS IN CHINA could be fearsome brigands. They could also be folk heros. Although they contain many examples of local bullies and highwaymen, Chinese stories about outlaws also make the point that the real criminals are officials and magistrates who manipulate the law for their own advantage. To be declared outside the law by the corrupt is not a mark of dishonour. To fight against it is an act of courage and defiance.

The most famous collection of such bandit stories is the late fourteenth or early fifteenth-century novel *The Legend of the Water Margin*, also known through Pearl S. Buck's translation as *All Men Are Brothers*. This remarkable work grew out of storytellers' repertoires over the centuries. In England, Robin Hood and his band of merry men camped in Sherwood Forest. Victims of injustice themselves, they helped the poor by targeting the rich and powerful. In China, 108 fugitives took refuge in a marshland at Liang Mountain in the northern province of Shandong. They too were victims of corruption, oppression, and injustice, and thirty-six of them are prominent characters in *The Legend of the Water Margin*.

Like Robin Hood, these outlaws became famous among common folk, who regarded them as heros. They successfully challenged authority; they possessed wonderful martial arts skills; they took pity on the helpless and wrought revenge against evil, rich, powerful officials; and they demonstrated great bravery. The band formed a microcosmic society with its own laws and code of behaviour which stood in contrast to the world around. The stories struck such a response in China that Liang Mountain is still primarily remembered as a bandit lair.

These tales make wonderful operas. They delight audiences with displays of martial arts and move them with dramatic stories of injustice, betrayal, and revenge. The outlaw heros of Liang Mountain have become deeply entrenched cultural icons, so potent a symbol of resistance against injustice that reading *The Legend of the Water Margin* was forbidden at various times in the Qing dynasty.

11.1
Wu Song, in Wu Song's Revenge. *Hebei Clapper opera*

Night Flight

夜奔

Hebei Clapper Opera

There is an old Chinese theatre saying: 'Actors fear *Night Flight.*' That this play has been singled out from others in such a demanding art form suggests that the piece asks a great deal of the performer. *Night Flight* requires the lead actor to use the complete range of his abilities. There are moments of difficult, dramatic singing and demonstrations of physical skills as the character battles a raging snowstorm. It is a virtuoso piece for the accomplished performer and the highlight of any opera program.

A military instructor, Lin Chong, was on the run. A powerful young lord with designs on Lin Chong's wife had falsely accused him of a crime and banished him far from home. But Lin Chong was too dangerous an enemy to let live. The young lord sent his henchmen to pursue the military instructor and frame him again for an even more serious offence. The local magistrate circulated drawings of the fugitive, posted a large reward for his capture, and sent out hundreds of soldiers to comb the countryside. Lin Chong had to flee for his life.

There was only one place to go. He had to make his way to the outlaws in the marsh at Liang Mountain. Lin Chong made the difficult journey at midnight, fighting a severe snowstorm all the way. When he thought he could manage the terrible journey no farther, he came to an old abandoned temple. He went inside for refuge and, seeing the likeness of the temple god, decided to pray for its patronage. If only the god would guide him safely to the mountain! Exhausted, Lin Chong fell asleep on the temple floor.

'Lin Chong! Wake up! You have no time for sleep!' Lin Chong saw that the image was alive and speaking to him with an urgent warning. 'A sharpshooter leading 500 soldiers is at the river crossing and almost upon you!' Lin Chong suddenly awoke and realized that the god of the temple had spoken to him in a dream. He bowed, thanked the image, and bolted from the temple.

Lin Chong sang of his sorrow as he forced himself onward, pressed by his pursuers behind and by the storm before. He lamented that he could not care for his mother or offer his talents to serve his country. His wife! What of his wife? What was going to happen to her? And what would now become of him? His heart burned in his despair and agony. Then, as he penetrated even deeper into the wilderness, he heard the sounds of wild animals surrounding him. Tigers snarled! Monkeys taunted him! Should he ever get to the outlaws' lair, he resolved, he would remember his suffering and wreak a terrible revenge on all who had ruined his life.

11.2
The fugitive Lin Chong grits his teeth in determination as he makes the difficult journey to the outlaws at Liang Mountain. Hebei Clapper opera

Li Kui Visits His Mother
李逵探母
Peking Opera

Li Kui was one of the most ferocious of the outlaws in the Liang Mountain lair. His nickname was Black Whirlwind because he was impulsive, violent, and emotional. No one could control him. Seeing that others of the outlaw band had brought their parents back to the lair, Li Kui was determined to bring back his old, sick mother. Knowing his temper, no one would accompany him. So he set out alone. Along the way, he met a bandit who robbed travellers and told everyone that he was the famous Black Whirlwind. The real Black Whirlwind battled this false one, but it was not much of a contest. Li Kui defeated him easily and killed him. He continued on his way without any further trouble.

Arriving home, Li Kui had a tearful reunion with his old mother. He discovered with shock that she was now blind, having cried daily for him in his life as an outlaw. She need cry no longer; he had come to take care of her. Carrying his mother on his back, Li Kui began the journey back to the Liang Mountain lair. The journey was a long and difficult one. He put his mother down to rest for a few moments and went to a stream to fetch water. When he came back, she was gone. A trail of blood led him to a grizzly discovery: a family of four tigers had killed and devoured his mother. The Black Whirlwind hurled himself against the tigers in a terrible rage and killed them all.

11.3
The Black Whirlwind, Li Kui, strikes a pose as he sets out on his journey. Peking opera

When the local villagers found that Li Kui had killed the tigers that had preyed on them for some time, they fêted him as their hero, preparing a great feast to express their gratitude. In attendance was none other than the wife of the false Black Whirlwind. She ran to the local magistrate to inform him that Li Kui was a wanted murderer and a famous outlaw of Liang Mountain marsh. She should earn a reward and revenge for her husband's death. The magistrate sent his officers, but they had to wait for the right moment to arrest such a fighter as Li Kui. When the Black Whirlwind was thoroughly drunk at the feast, the magistrate's men tied him up and led him away captive. It would have been the end of Li Kui, but news of his capture got back to Liang Mountain. The outlaws launched a rescue, drugging the guards' food and drink. Li Kui was able to return to the safety of the outlaw lair.

11.4
The proud and powerful outlaw has a tearful reunion with his sick, blind mother. Peking opera

Li Kui Visits His Mother

Wu Song's Revenge
武松血濺鴛鴦樓
Hebei Clapper Opera

Wu Song had earned the secure post of officer in the infantry because of his marvellous fighting skills. Everyone knew how he had single-handedly killed a ferocious tiger that had devoured many people. He was a hero. But his good fortune was not to last. One day, Wu Song turned himself in to the magistrate and confessed to killing his sister-in-law and her lover on learning that they had murdered his brother. The magistrate knew Wu Song to be an upright man but could not ignore a double killing even if it was in revenge. He sentenced Wu Song to exile in the far-off city of Mengzhou, the setting for *Wu Song's Revenge.*

He found life in Mengzhou more pleasant than he had imagined. The jailer's son befriended him and frequently invited him to feasts. Why was he, a branded criminal, getting such good treatment? It turned out that the jailer's son had a job for him. A brawling brigand named Jiang the Gate God had seized a wine shop belonging to the jailer's son. No one could do anything about him. He was as large and as fearsome as the guardian gods painted on temple doors – hence his name. Who could handle that? Wu Song the Tiger Killer's reputation had preceded him. He was the only hope to get rid of Jiang. After hearing the story, Wu Song promised to kill Jiang just as he had done the tiger and set out with the jailer's son. Wu Song's courage and strength were always brought out by good wine, so the jailer's son plied him with drink along the way. When he arrived at the shop, Wu Song's face was flushed with strong drink. He was ready for a fight! He tossed the waiters about and into the wine vats. He tore up the tavern and then sought out Jiang the Gate God, whom he roundly defeated. Jiang, humiliated, was made to

promise to apologize and leave for good.

The news that Wu Song had so easily accomplished what no other could do spread quickly. The local general invited this new hero to join his staff. General Zhang Mengfang treated Wu Song like a son and gave him the run of his mansion. But one night, Wu Song suddenly found himself in chains. Guards had searched his room and found it full of precious treasures that had recently disappeared from the general's rooms. Zhang Mengfang was furious. How dare his new recruit betray the general's trust! Wu Song was thrown into a dungeon, his head locked into a rack.

For the second time, Wu Song found himself escorted by guards to distant exile. Along the way he met his friend the jailer's son. But what was this? Why was his friend so severely beaten and heavily bandaged? The jailer's son told Wu Song that Jiang the Gate God was back. The whole affair was an elaborate trick. Jiang had fled after his defeat to a friend, a high official. That official's sworn blood brother was none other than General Zhang Mengfang, and the magistrate who had sentenced Wu Song was in the official's pay. It was now clear. The general's kind invitation, the run of the mansion, and Wu Song's promotion were simply parts of a plot to frame him as a thief. With Wu Song out of the way, Jiang could have free rein again.

Wu Song continued on in chains to his exile but became suspicious when extra armed guards joined his escort. He took his chance at the bridge over Flying Cloud Pool. Suddenly, he lashed out at the guards with his feet and smashed the rack about his neck. Within moments, he had killed all the guards but one, from whom he forced the confession that

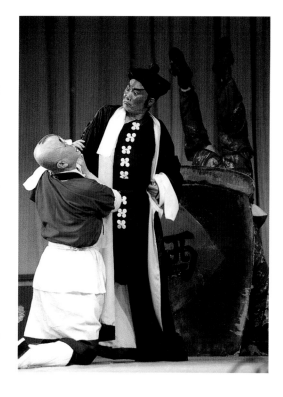

11.5
Wu Song, his face flushed with strong drink, tosses the waiters into the wine vat. Hebei Clapper opera

General Zhang Mengfang had ordered them to kill Wu Song along the way. Even now, the general, the official, the magistrate, and Jiang the Gate God were feasting in the general's great hall, waiting for the happy news of Wu Song's murder. Wu Song killed the last guard, turned about, and resolutely headed back to Mengzhou.

He arrived late at night and gained entry to the general's mansion by climbing over a wall. After threatening a guard at dagger point, Wu Song learned the general's whereabouts. He broke into the great hall to find the conspirators drinking and eating to celebrate the success of their plan. Shocked and confused at Wu Song's appearance, they tried to resist, but no one was a match for the Tiger Killer. Wu Song killed each one of them and cut off their heads. Dipping a strip of cloth in their blood he boldly wrote on the wall: The killer of these men was Wu Song the Tiger Killer! Indeed, this Tiger Killer would go on to join the famous band of Liang Mountain and become one of its most celebrated outlaws.

11.6
Having freed himself and killed the guards at the bridge, Wu Song prepares to exact revenge. Hebei Clapper opera

Wu Song's Revenge

11.7
*Early in the story, the Tiger Killer easily defeats
Jiang the Gate God, who is shocked to meet such a
powerful opponent. Hebei Clapper opera*

11.8
*A terrified guard in the general's mansion tells Wu
Song where the plotters are gathered. Hebei
Clapper opera*

11.9 *(facing page)*
*After the slaughter, Wu Song signs his name in the
blood of his enemies. Hebei Clapper opera*

Wu Song's Revenge

Chapter 12   Ghosts

IT IS REMARKABLE how many Chinese ghost stories are about justice. The stage often portrays the grim experience of injustice in this world but gives the audience the satisfaction of seeing wrongs made right from the next. Redress can come about in a number of ways. Ghosts can work through the dreams of mortals or return to the world themselves for revenge. Some return to life, while others drag the living back to the spirit world with them. The poor and the powerless are justified among the spirits. At the mercy of the corrupt and the violent in this world, they come back as awesome spectres, able to carry off even high officials to the dark regions.

The world of ghosts is much more fair than this one. In fact, existence among ghosts begins with a general accounting. When you die, your spirit goes directly to the underworld to face King Yanlo. He has a great book in which is recorded the life of every individual. If you have passed the life meant for you, then you take your place among the spirits. If you have not, King Yanlo (also called King Yama) will find it out immediately. He might send you back to earth in order to give you the time that is rightfully yours if he discovers that your life was prematurely cut short. He might allow you to seek out the partner whom fate decreed for you but with whom you never fulfilled your destiny. If you were a scholar cheated out of a deserved official's position in the world of the living, you might find yourself appointed governor of ghosts.

But as a ghost, you lose something of your humanity. Transformed, you are separated from all living creatures. The Chinese stage shows that transformation and separation by strange, deliberately askew make-up and displays of superhuman powers such as fire breathing. Ghosts might accomplish their revenge, obtain justice, or clear their names, but they still stand outside the kind of happiness possible in the living world unless they return to it as fully human again. The human world can be re-entered by means other than the Buddhist doctrine of reincarnation, as we see in two of the plays below.

12.1
The wandering spirit of Li Huiniang, in Sorrow at West Lake. *Qin opera*

Zhong Kui Arranges a Marriage
鍾馗嫁妹
Hebei Clapper Opera

Who is the real demon: a spectre from the next world or a corrupt oppressor of the innocent in this one? *Zhong Kui Arranges a Marriage* uses a supernatural visitation from the world of ghosts to put this question. It is a play about injustice and oppression on the one hand and love and friendship on the other. The images of this opera are particularly striking. An army of ghosts forming a marriage procession makes a powerful contrast between life and death. The ghostly demons are terrifying and dangerous, but only to the human demons who fill the world with corruption and suffering. Zhong Kui's return to the world to arrange his sister's wedding is an act of tender, brotherly concern for her and an expression of esteem for his friend. A lone,

penniless woman in China with no one to speak for her had no options. She would need a miracle from the other world. The highlight of this opera is the bizarre journey of Zhong Kui and his retinue of ghosts from his tomb to his old home. It is a breathtaking performance of acrobatics and stage effects accompanied by furious gongs and drums.

Zhong Kui and his sister were desperately poor. Their parents had died early, leaving the two to fend for themselves. Zhong Kui, a talented scholar, refused to take the official exams because the system was corrupt. Without money and influence he could not hope for impartial treatment. His only recourse was to eke out a meagre living by copying

scrolls. All this changed when the local magistrate's son, an insufferable bully, tried to force Zhong Kui's sister to marry him and to coerce Zhong Kui into writing the exams using the son's name. Zhong Kui saw no way out. He must go to the capital and write the exams under his own name. If he succeeded, he and his sister could escape poverty and oppression.

The system was as corrupt as Zhong Kui feared. The chief examiner was related to the magistrate's son. When he saw how badly the son had done on the exams, he switched names with the most brilliant graduate – Zhong Kui. Zhong Kui protested, threatening to expose this corruption, but the examiner indignantly ordered his arrest. In an act of defiance and desperation, Zhong Kui smashed his head against a pillar and died. Du Ping, a fellow scholar whom Zhong Kui had befriended on the way to the exam, mourned the death of this good man and gave him proper burial.

The examination official was outraged. Had he not ordered that this troublemaker should go without burial? How dare Du Ping defy him! The official led troops to the tomb to arrest the still-mourning Du Ping. Suddenly, a deep voice called out from the grave. It was Zhong Kui, transformed into a horrific apparition! Deprived of his right to an official position in this world, he was now an official of ghosts and demons in the next. A whole army of ghosts emerged

12.2
Zhong Kui, in the simple make-up of a young man's role, grabs hold of the wicked chief examiner, swearing to come back as a ghost to deal with demons like him who cause so much suffering in the world. Hebei Clapper opera

from the tomb, defeated the soldiers, and carried off the terrified chief examiner.

The ghost of Zhong Kui now turned his
attention to Du Ping. His good friend had
risked his life to give him burial. Now Zhong
Kui would express his gratitude by arranging a
marriage with his sister. Was Du Ping willing?
More than willing. So Zhong Kui and his ghosts
set out on a journey of hundreds of miles over
mountains and rivers to bring a dowry to his
sister. The ghosts playfully mimicked a wedding procession, one wearing the red marriage
veil of a bride. They crossed valleys in somer-
saults and backflips, all the while shouldering
their packages or carrying Zhong Kui's official
umbrella. Zhong Kui himself flipped over
backward from a height and landed on the
ground, performing splits and other gymnas-
tics. Standing on the back of one of his ghosts,
he breathed fire in a demonstration of his
ghostly powers. Finally, the procession arrived
at the door of Zhong Kui's old home.

His sister was tremendously excited to hear
his voice outside the door, for the bully was on
his way to force the marriage! She froze in horror when she saw the transformed Zhong Kui,
but as he told her his story, she wept for her
poor brother. She was moved that he had come
back from the grave to see her married and
cared for. Of course she would agree to the
marriage!

12.3
*Zhong Kui journeys in a ghostly procession from
the underworld. His make-up shows that he has
become a fearsome spectre, but his headdress
indicates that he is now also an official. Hebei
Clapper opera*

Zhong Kui Arranges a Marriage

The magistrate's son walked in demanding that she become his wife. 'A demon!' he cried in horror when he saw the imposing Zhong Kui. 'Who is the real demon?' retorted the ghost. 'It is you who are the demon of this world!' Zhong Kui's ghosts swept up the petrified bully and dragged him to hell.

Zhong Kui and his ghosts led the sister in an eerie marriage procession to Du Ping. Now that he had accomplished his hopes for his sister and friend, Zhong Kui ascended into the world of the spirits. Denied happiness for himself, he had ensured it for those he loved.

12.4 (facing page)
Zhong Kui mounts a black horse, his black tasselled riding crop, steadied by a kneeling demon. He is leading an army of ghosts to his old home and bringing a dowry for his sister. Hebei Clapper opera

12.5
The elevated shoes, padded shoulders, enlarged face, and gigantic fan all make the ghostly official formidable and larger than life. Hebei Clapper opera

12.6
*Zhong Kui, leading the wedding procession in high
spirits, marries off his sister to Du Ping. Hebei
Clapper opera*

The Haunting of Zhang Sanlang
活捉三郎
Sichuan Opera

The Haunting of Zhang Sanlang is a comic ghost story. Zhang Sanlang is a clown role with the characteristic small white patch on the face. He sings drunken songs and mistakenly identifies a ghost as one of his many girlfriends; he performs stunts while running away from the ghost and manipulates his costume to convey his terror. Zhang Sanlang is a ridiculous figure, unworthy of the journey that a ghost has taken for him.

The story comes from the Ming dynasty novel *The Legend of the Water Margin.* In it, one of the outlaw heroes rescues a woman,

Yan Xijiao, from destitution. Later, she takes a lover behind his back and attempts to blackmail the outlaw with proof of his identity. Angry at her ingratitude and fearful that he will be exposed, the outlaw murders her. The opera tells what happens after the murder.

Yan Xijiao was dead. Her lover, Zhang Sanlang, knew that she had been murdered but it was all the same to him. He had had affairs before and doubtless would again. Yan Xijiao, however, had loved him with a love transcending life and death. Her ghost pleaded its case in the underworld and won permission to return

to the living. She would go to Zhang Sanlang and bring him back with her so that they might live together among the spirits.

Zhang Sanlang was sleeping it off after a night of carousing. Abruptly, a voice awakened him. He became most interested when he realized that there was a woman outside his door who wanted to come in. Which one of his many girlfriends had come to him in the middle of the night? Zhang Sanlang lit a candle and eagerly opened the door. He was horrified when a spectre appeared in his room, though she told him not to be afraid. She was Yan Xijiao, who loved him so much that she had come back from the grave to fetch him. If they could not find happiness in this world, they would find it as husband and wife in the underworld. Yan Xijiao did not expect his response. 'Get out or I will call for help,' screamed the quivering young man. 'It was all just a game before. It didn't mean anything!'

The ghost was enraged at his faithlessness. She scolded and threatened her former lover until he turned black with dread and fear. Zhang Sanlang tried to flee, but the ghost blocked his every escape. Finally, Yan Xijiao caught him, hanged him, and led him off to join her in the world of the dead forever.

12.7
Yan Xijiao, wearing a mask, is delighted to tell the quivering Zhang Sanlang that the king of the underworld has allowed her to come back to earth to get him. Now, they can live happily together among the dead. Sichuan opera

12.8 (facing page)
Zhang Sanlang, in clown white-face, finds a ghost
in his room in the dead of night. Sichuan opera

12.9
Zhang Sanlang tries to escape, but there is
nowhere to hide from a ghost. Yan Xijiao prepares
to catch him in her silken scarf. Sichuan opera

Red Plum Blossoms
再世紅梅記
Qin and Cantonese Opera

A concubine in the mansion of a powerful official had no life of her own. She was free neither to go out nor to make any choices without her master's permission. It is not surprising, then, how important love at first sight is in Chinese stories. Opportunities and experiences were few for such a woman, and she had to take love and happiness where and when she found it. The Qin opera *Sorrow at West Lake* and the Cantonese opera *Red Plum Blossoms* tell the same story of a woman in such restricted circumstances. *Red Plum Blossoms*, in particular, offers striking moments of staging, special effects, and acting, as the story involves pleasure boating, fire spitting, and a mad scene.

The young scholar Pei Yu was enjoying a holiday. He had just passed the exams with highest honours and was now entitled to become an official in the palace. To celebrate, he invited his friends out boating on Hangzhou's famous West Lake. The scheming official Jia Sidao was also out boating that day with his concubines. The most beautiful of them was Li Huiniang, of whom the official was extremely jealous. The two boats drifted close together and bumped into each other. Scholar Pei Yu quickly opened his window to see what had happened. As he looked out, he saw Li Huiniang opening the window shutters of the other boat. The two fell in love instantly but not unbeknown to Jia Sidao, who had observed everything. The jealous official waited until he and his concubines had returned to his mansion. Once there he summoned Li Huiniang and killed her with a sword as an example to the others. Jia Sidao ordered her body buried beneath a red plum tree and her head kept in a box inside the mansion's Red Plum Chamber.

Li Huiniang's spirit descended to the under-

world to be judged by King Yanlo. He was surprised when he consulted his great book of life to find that she was not supposed to be dead at all. She had seventy-two years coming to her, not sixteen. The book further declared that she had been fated to be the wife of Scholar Pei Yu. To partly redress this terrible wrong, the king gave her a magic fan to take her back to the world of the living for a hundred days. She returned, eager to seek out the young scholar.

Scholar Pei Yu, however, had run into troubles of his own. Trying to pluck a red plum blossom, he had fallen over a wall into a private garden. There he was surprised to see a beautiful young woman, Lu Zhaorong, who was the image of Li Huiniang. The evil official

also knew of Lu Zhaorong and was determined to have her take the place of his murdered concubine. What was Lu Zhaorong to do? She begged the young scholar for help.

He concocted a plan in which Lu Zhaorong was to feign insanity and then fly to the city of Yangzhou. Pei Yu visited Jia Sidao in the guise of a new graduate paying respects to a high official. Jia Sidao was at first displeased with the scholar not only because of his infatuation with Li Huiniang but also because he had taken so long to pay his courtesy call. But then Pei Yu explained his delay. His brother had become mad from an infatuation with a mad woman. Jia Sidao told him that word had come that his intended concubine had lost her mind. Perhaps the young scholar could use his experience to help him judge whether or not she was truly mad.

Lu Zhaorong and her father were brought to the official's mansion. Her clothes and hair were in disarray. Seeing Jia Sidao, she fell on her knees in obeisance calling him Yanlo, king of the underworld. Scholar Pei Yu advised the official that it was a dangerous thing to take in a woman who could not differentiate between this world and the next. Lu Zhaorong then began to talk of her husband. It seemed she was no longer a maiden. 'Who is your husband?' demanded Jia Sidao. 'He is,' said Lu Zhaorong pointing to Pei Yu, 'and he,' pointing to her father. A shocking thing for any young Chinese woman to say!

Jia Sidao decided on a test. He called for a club to beat the old man. Her reaction would tell him the truth. At first she did not seem to care, but then began to laugh at the beating. Rushing over, she seized the club so she could get in a few strokes herself. 'Enough!' said the official. 'Take her away!' But Lu Zhaorong would not go. Why would the king of the underworld call her only to send her back? Scholar Pei Yu hastily intervened, offering to coax her away quietly. Jia Sidao was relieved to be rid of her, and invited Pei Yu to return that evening so that he could thank the scholar.

12.10 *(facing page)*
Scholar Pei Yu falls over a wall into a garden while trying to pick a red plum blossom and sees a beautiful woman who is the image of Li Huiniang. Cantonese opera

12.11
Lu Zhaorong pretends to be insane to escape the wicked official Jia Sidao. Cantonese opera

But Jia Sidao's nephew later reported that he had seen Scholar Pei Yu hiding in Lu Zhaorong's garden. Moreover, on leaving the official's mansion the two had been whispering like conspirators. Jia Sidao realized that he had been tricked. He was resolved to imprison the scholar in his mansion when he returned and have him put to death.

That very night, Li Huiniang arrived in the world and came to Pei Yu. She declared her love and told him that he was in great danger. An assassin was coming for him, but she would protect him. Revealing that she was a ghost from the underworld, she breathed fire and used her ghostly powers to terrify the would-be murderer, who had crept into the garden. She forced her tormentor, the official, against the wall, and saved the young scholar. The ghost then took him away to Yangzhou to the bedside of Lu Zhaorong, who had died from illness. The ghost entered the young woman's body, and Li Huiniang opened her eyes. She was back in the flesh, with a second chance for love and happiness with Scholar Pei Yu.

Red Plum Blossoms

12.12 (facing page)
The ghost stands ready to defend Pei Yu from the
assassin in the garden. Qin opera

12.13
The ghost breathes fire and waves a magic fan to
terrify the would-be murderer. Qin opera

The Wrath of the Fox Fairy
狐仙恨
Sichuan Opera

Fox fairies are formidable spirits. They can raise fire by striking their tails on the ground and transform themselves into human beings, usually maidens. An early Qing dynasty collection of fantastic tales, *Strange Stories from the Make-Do Studio,* includes encounters with these creatures. The Sichuan opera draws many of its fox fairy stories from that collection. These operas are so popular that there is a special fox fairy role type for young performers. Fox fairy maidens can make loving, devoted wives. They can also make terrifying opponents if crossed. One always treads carefully with a fox fairy.

Shi Huaiyu was a poor scholar. His one great fortune was a thoughtful, loving wife who shared all his struggles with him. She had complete confidence that one day he would excel at the exams and obtain a high position. That great day finally came. Shi Huaiyu obtained top graduate honours and instantly became a success. Every high official with a marriageable daughter had his eye on the graduate. He was delighted at all the new prospects that were opening up to him, but there was one problem. His wife was an embarrassment, an obstacle to his marrying into a great family. Now that his fortunes had changed for the better, he just could not let these opportunities slip through his fingers. So he murdered her.

What Shi Huaiyu did not know, however, was that his loyal, loving wife was actually a fox fairy. She was not dead but came back to him with all the fury of an outraged spirit. The fox fairy wanted to exact her own justice for his ingratitude and betrayal. Shi Huaiyu cowered in horror as the fox spirit whirled about him. His face turned blacker and blacker as she closed in. There was no escape. Finally, she finished toying with him and grabbed hold.

12.15
Shi Huaiyu's face begins to turn black with fear as the fox fairy overwhelms him. Sichuan opera

12.14
Shi Huaiyu wears his brand new robes of office but holds a sword to kill his wife, who represents an obstacle to even greater honours. Sichuan opera

12.16 (facing page)
The fox fairy returns for vengeance. Shi Huaiyu cannot escape from such a powerful being, and his face turns black with terror. Sichuan opera

The Wrath of the Fox Fairy

The Peony Pavilion
牡丹亭驚夢
Cantonese Opera

The Peony Pavilion is not just a ghost story but a story of death and resurrection. A young woman, Du Liniang, finds love in a dream, waits for it as a spirit, and reaches out to claim it from the dead. The play was written in 1598 by the master dramatist Tang Xianzu. He wove together a number of themes in this complex work of over fifty scenes that took days to perform. The Cantonese opera version presented here was written in 1956 by Tang Disheng. He reworked the original into a taut eight scenes that could be performed in a single evening.

Du Liniang lived in a great house with gardens and courtyards. Her family had wealth and position, but she was not happy. Like any proper young lady, she was largely confined to her family home. She felt imprisoned in the great house; her youth was as fleeting as the spring and it was wasting away! How would she ever find love? Du Liniang, accompanied by her maid, went to the peony pavilion in the garden to try to relieve her melancholy. She fell asleep and dreamed a wonderful dream. In it, a handsome young man, Liu Mengmei, came to her carrying a willow branch. He tugged at the young maiden's sleeve, whispering that they were destined to be together. Du Liniang's heart beat wildly as he led her beneath a willow tree. The leaves and the flowers, he said, would hide them. But a falling blossom awakened the young girl and ended her dream. She could not endure this life any longer. She was heartsick for the young man, and her health failed. Knowing that she would die soon, she painted a portrait of herself and wrote a poem concealing the name Liu Mengmei.

Three years later, a blizzard forced a young scholar on his way to try the exams at the capital to stop at a small temple. His name was Liu Mengmei. He asked the two nuns in charge if he could have shelter for the night. Once inside, he offered up incense to the divinity to which the temple was dedicated. At first he thought it was a picture of the Goddess of Mercy. It was, in fact, the portrait of Du Liniang. Liu Mengmei had chanced on a shrine built to her memory by her family, who had moved far away. Liu Mengmei read the poem on the painting and realized with a shock that it referred to him. What could it mean? Du Liniang appeared to him and told him the whole story. Liu Mengmei now knew that she had died for love of him.

But there was still a chance for happiness. The king of the underworld had discovered in his great book that Liu Mengmei and Du Liniang were fated to be husband and wife. He therefore granted her permission to return to the living the following day. The ghost instructed Liu Mengmei to open her tomb before noon. If he failed, she would lose her only chance for life. The next day, Liu Mengmei began to dig at the tomb. The nuns were horrified at the sacrilege, but when the young scholar flung the tomb open Du Liniang walked out alive and human again.

The couple set out together, first for Liu Mengmei to write the civil exams and then to seek Du Liniang's parents. They needed and wanted the older couple's blessing for the marriage. The lovers managed to convince Du Liniang's mother, but her father refused to believe Liu Mengmei and ordered him beaten as a lunatic. When he saw Du Liniang, he was convinced that she was a ghost and ordered his gates barred against her.

Finally, the case was brought before the emperor himself. Liu Mengmei protested that he was neither crazy nor a tomb robber. The beautiful Du Liniang had indeed risen from the dead; she was no ghost. The emperor called out priests and monks to test her. A ghost would not be able to face them. When it was apparent to everyone that Du Liniang was not a ghost, her father accused her of being a demon in disguise. The emperor then ordered her to look into a demon mirror, which would reflect her true likeness. When she did, everyone could see that it showed only the face of the beautiful young girl. Du Liniang's father finally accepted the truth and, on learning that Liu Mengmei had passed the exam with top honours, consented to the marriage.

12.17 (facing page)
Lovesick over the man she met in a dream, Du Liniang paints her own portrait and writes a cryptic poem before she dies. Cantonese opera

12.18
*The ghost of Du Liniang appears to the young
scholar in his room. Cantonese opera*

12.19 *(facing page)*
*Liu Mengmei discovers the portrait three years later
and ponders the meaning of the poem, which clearly
implies his name. Did he not once have a dream
about this beautiful maiden? Cantonese opera*

The Peony Pavilion

A Woodshed Encounter
柴房會
Chaozhou Opera

Li Laosan the pedlar is a clown's role. The clown is featured in the Chaozhou opera and much admired for his acrobatic skills. *A Woodshed Encounter* begins with the physical comedy of a terrified clown and continues with the verbal comedy of his interrogation of a ghost. The play ends, however, on a note of sympathy and generosity for a young girl who has suffered betrayal and hardship her whole life.

Li Laosan was an itinerant pedlar. One particular night, he settled down in the woodshed of a small inn. Just as he was about to lie down, an apparition suddenly appeared before him. A ghost! Li Laosan was terrified and tried to escape by scrambling up a ladder. But then he noticed a very strange thing: the ghost was crying. It was a pretty young girl in great despair. What could this mean? Li Laosan slowly descended the ladder and decided to address the spectre.

'Don't cry. Tell me your story,' he said to the ghost. And she did. The ghost had once been a girl named Mo Erniang. Her parents had died early in life leaving her and an elder brother alone. The brother was a wastrel who thought only of gambling and drinking, but those habits needed money and they were very poor. So, looking about him, he sold the one commodity he had, his young sister. Mo Erniang was horrified to find herself sold to a brothel to support her brother's habits, but there was nothing she could do.

'Well,' said Li Laosan. 'That was fine! You could dress up beautifully every day, attract rich young men, and trick them out of all their cash!' The ghost cried out that it was agony. The madam was very severe and had beaten her at the slightest provocation. One day, however, a handsome young merchant, Yang Chun,

and his brother came to the brothel. Yang Chun was so taken with Mo Erniang that he stayed with her, and the two quickly fell in love. For the first time in her life she began to experience happiness. Not long after, Yang Chun ran out of money and the madam's demeanour changed just as suddenly as the merchant's fortune. She threw out the two men. Mo Erniang could not bear to lose Yang Chun and ran away to join him, but she became ill on the road and could not travel well. What's more, Yang Chun seemed somehow changed to her. Her uneasiness proved all too justified when he sold her to a shopkeeper, a horrible man who planned to make Mo

Erniang his wife. Having spent their money at the brothel, Yang Chun and his brother had decided that selling her was the only way to recover their losses. Unable to endure any more, she hanged herself. Now, her ghost was back in the world seeking justice for all that she had suffered.

Li Laosan was deeply moved by the story and indignant at how Mo Erniang had been betrayed in life. He would go with the ghost to seek out the vile Yang Chun and send him off to the underworld to answer for his crimes. The ghost cried out in joy that Li Laosan was her benefactor. And so the two set out to accomplish their revenge.

12.20 *(facing page)*
The ghost, in white and holding an umbrella to signify that she is going on a journey, is grateful to Li Laosan, who is moved by her sad story and has agreed to help. Chaozhou opera

12.21
Li Laosan scrambles up a ladder. It's a ghost! His white make-up and moustache clearly identify him as a clown, a main fixture of Chaozhou opera. Chaozhou opera

Chapter 13   A Final Word

CACOPHONY! This book started out with a Westerner seeing a Chinese opera for the first time. It was a Peking opera in this collection, *The Warrior Maiden Mu Guiying*, in which a warrior woman battles a young general. That particular performance, given by the amateur Chinese Opera Group of Toronto, took place in 1993 at a Toronto festival open to the general public. When the orchestra really got going with its drums, gongs, and cymbals, it came as a shock for many Western ears. The intensity, the volume, and the energy were overwhelming, and several people sat through it with their fingers in their ears. Someone commented that it sounded as if all the kitchen pots and pans had been brought out. A 1970s Toronto newspaper review of a visiting professional troupe from China made similar comments. When it came to the singing style of the female role, the *qingyi*, the reviewer said that it was best compared to a woman singing while sitting on a block of ice. Typically, students just starting to learn about performing arts in China will say that their impression of Chinese opera is noise and fighting. But these are starting points. A little effort is needed to get past them.

There is a stage language quite apart from speech that opens up Chinese opera to reveal a sophisticated theatre executed by highly trained artists. Learning that language of conventions is very rewarding. The spectator not only follows the sense of the play but also discovers a remarkable treasure – the synthesis of China's arts, history, philosophy, and religions all in one package. It is no longer pots and pans or a woman on ice. The Chinese opera, in all its regional variations, is now both pleasurable and of immense value. *Chinese Opera* is intended to convey some of that.

At one of the many meetings that went into this book, the publisher observed that if nothing else, preserving Siu Wang-Ngai's photographs and making them available was an important service for the future. He was referring to a growing problem, the decline of traditional opera in China. In a country focused on modernizing itself and growing financially, there is a shrinking audience for the old musical systems and the old stories. Many Chinese do not know the conventions of classical opera, and find Western-style popular music, television, and film far more accessible and relevant to a changing country.

Governments in mainland China, Taiwan, and other Chinese communities bolster traditional opera in a number of ways. They sponsor live and broadcast

13.1
The young 'widow' and her husband, in The Young Widow at the Grave. *Peking opera*

performances and support troupes and training schools. The military, for example, has its own Peking opera companies. The danger is that classical opera is not so much fostered as preserved, a very different thing. To foster is to encourage growth as part of a tradition formed by a close relationship with the audience. When the audience is largely lost and what remains is for the most part an older generation, the opera stops growing. Younger audiences already regard it as something of a museum piece. When that process happened to *kunqu,* regional forms filled the gap, and gradually one of them, Peking opera, emerged as a major theatrical style. Now Peking opera is going the same way as *kunqu,* but in the electronic age it is unlikely that some regional opera style will captivate the general public. Nonetheless, regional opera forms do continue to have their following because they are bound up with dialect and local identity. But regional opera, too, has lost much of its audience.

Theatrical artists are trying a number of experiments with Chinese opera to attract audiences and to keep it part of a living tradition. Many of these efforts combine elements of electronic media and Western performance art with Chinese traditional performance technique. Two plays in this collection, *The Hibiscus Fairy* and *Cao Cao and Yang Xiu,* are good examples. It is significant that both these productions were enthusiastically received by large audiences. The photographs in this book and the stories that accompany them demonstrate both the tradition and the modern development of Chinese regional opera.

Appendix A: English Guide to Photographs

Photo	Genre	Opera	Troupe	Characters	Performers	Year
p. ii	Sichuan	*Delights of the Mortal World*	Chengdu Hibiscus Sichuan Opera Troupe	White Eel Fairy	Yu Haiyan	1988
1.1	Longjiang	*The Imperial Kinsmen*	Heilongjiang Provincial Longjiang Opera Experimental Theatre	Bai Mang Shen Mende Old Lady Wei Gao	Li Ruigang Gao Yuncheng Lü Dongmei Zhao Youshan	1991
3.5	Peking	*Qin Xianglian*	Tianjin Youth Beijing Opera Troupe	Qin Xianglian	Lei Ying	1987
3.6	Yue	*The Pearl Hairpin*	Zhejiang Little Flowers Shaoxing Opera Troupe	Huo Dingjin	He Saifei	1990
3.7	Peking	*The Young Widow at the Grave*	Liaoling Youth Beijing Opera Troupe	Xiao Suzhen	Guan Bo	1986
3.8	Jiangxi	*Jumping into Fire*	Jiangxi Gan Opera Troupe	Jie Zhitui Jie's Mother	Li Weide Chen Xiaoxia	1992
3.9	Peking	*Gift at Rainbow Bridge*	Shenyang Beijing Opera Theatre	Water Fairy	Li Jingwen	1993
3.10	Jiangxi	*Choosing a Warhorse*	Jiangxi Gan Opera Troupe	Mu Guiying	Chen Li	1992
3.11	Yue	*The Pearl Hairpin*	Zhejiang Little Flowers Shaoxing Opera Troupe	Wen Bizheng	Xia Saili	1990
3.12	Cantonese	*The Peony Pavilion*	Chor Fung Ming Cantonese Opera Troupe	Du Bao	Lang Chi-Pak	1985
3.13	Kunqu	*Splendour Chamber*	Chinese Kunqu Opera Artists Troupe	Li Cunxiao	Wang Zhiquan	1989
3.14	Peking	*The Changban Slopes*	Tianjin Youth Beijing Opera Troupe	Zhao Yun	Wang Lijun	1987
3.15	Peking	*Qin Xianglian*	Tianjin Youth Beijing Opera Troupe	Bao Zheng	Meng Guanglu	1987
3.16	Sichuan	*Pi Jin Plays the Fool*	Chengdu Hibiscus Sichuan Opera Troupe	Pi Jin	Su Mingde	1988
3.17	Yue	*The Story of He Wenxiu*	Zhejiang Little Flowers Shaoxing Opera Troupe	Mother Yang	Yu Huizhen	1990
4.1	Sichuan	*The Legend of the White Snake*	Chengdu Hibiscus Sichuan Opera Troupe	God of Fire Weituo Begging Bowl Spirit Heng and Ha	Unknown	1988
4.2	Sichuan	*The Hibiscus Fairy*	Chengdu Hibiscus Sichuan Opera Troupe	Hibiscus Fairy	Yu Haiyan	1988
4.3	Sichuan	*The Hibiscus Fairy*	Chengdu Hibiscus Sichuan Opera Troupe	Hibiscus Fairy	Yu Haiyan	1988
4.4	Sichuan	*The Hibiscus Fairy*	Chengdu Hibiscus Sichuan Opera Troupe	Hibiscus Fairy Chen Qiulin	Yu Haiyan Chen Zhilin	1988
4.5	Sichuan	*The Hibiscus Fairy*	Chengdu Hibiscus Sichuan Opera Troupe	Banana Spirit	Yang Yongjie	1988
4.6	Sichuan	*The Legend of the White Snake*	Chengdu Sichuan Opera Theatre No. 3 Company	Blue Snake White Snake	Liu Ping Chen Qiaoru	1991
4.7	Sichuan	*The Legend of the White Snake*	Chengdu Hibiscus Sichuan Opera Troupe	White Snake Blue Snake	Li Sha Tu Tiejun	1988

Photo	Genre	Opera	Troupe	Characters	Performers	Year
4.8	Sichuan	*The Legend of the White Snake*	Chengdu Sichuan Opera Theatre No. 3 Company	Xu Xian Fahai White Snake Blue Snake Wang Daoling	Sun Yongbo Sun Puxie Chen Qiaoru Zhu Jianguo Li Zenglin	1991
4.9	Sichuan	*The Legend of the White Snake*	Chengdu Sichuan Opera Theatre No. 3 Company	Begging Bowl Spirit	Xiao Ting	1991
4.10	Anhui	*The Legend of the White Snake*	Anhui Provincial Hui Opera Troupe	White Snake Xu Xian Blue Snake	Luo Liping Li Taishan Jia Yiping	1991
4.11	Chaozhou	*The Legend of the White Snake*	Guangdong Chaozhou Opera Troupe	White Snake Xu Xian	Zeng Fu Zhong Yikun	1984
4.12	Peking	*The Eight Immortals Cross the Sea*	Liaoling Youth Beijing Opera Troupe	Zhong Liquan Lan Caihe He Xiangu Li Tieguai Zhang Guolao Cao Guojiu	Ma Zhengguang Zhang Wei Wang Yulan Jiang Daguang Chang Jing Luo Yichun	1986
4.13	Peking	*The Eight Immortals Cross the Sea*	Liaoling Youth Beijing Opera Troupe	Goldfish Fairy	Xue Junqiu	1986
4.14	Peking	*The Eight Immortals Cross the Sea*	Liaoling Youth Beijing Opera Troupe	Goldfish Fairy	Xue Junqiu	1986
4.15	Peking	*The Eight Immortals Cross the Sea*	Liaoling Youth Beijing Opera Troupe	Lü Dongbin Goldfish Fairy	Wu Kun Xue Junqiu	1986
4.16	Anhui	*Crossing Wits*	Anhui Provincial Hui Opera Troupe	Lü Dongbin	Cao Shangli	1991
4.17	Anhui	*Crossing Wits*	Anhui Provincial Hui Opera Troupe	White Peony	Li Xiaohong	1991
4.18	Hebei Clapper	*Monkey Business in Heaven*	Hebei Clapper Opera Troupe	Sun Wukong	Pei Yanling	1992
4.19	Peking	*Monkey Business in Heaven*	Tianjin Youth Beijing Opera Troupe	Heavenly Warrior Sun Wukong	Chen Xiqiang Shi Xiaoliang	1990
4.20	Shaoxing	*Monkey Steals the Magic Fan*	Zhejiang Provincial Shaoxing Shao Opera Troupe	Sun Wukong Pigsy	Liu Jianyang Qixiaoling Tong	1991
4.21	Shaoxing	*Monkey Steals the Magic Fan*	Zhejiang Provincial Shaoxing Shao Opera Troupe	Sun Wukong	Liu Jianyang	1991
4.22	Shaoxing	*Monkey and the White Bone Demon*	Zhejiang Provincial Shaoxing Shao Opera Troupe	White Bone Demon	Sun Xiaoyan	1991
4.23	Shaoxing	*Monkey and the White Bone Demon*	Zhejiang Provincial Shaoxing Shao Opera Troupe	Xuanzang Old Man	Wang Zhenfang Zhong Guoliang	1991
4.24	Peking	*Monkey and the Cave of Spiders*	Shanghai Beijing Opera Theatre	Pigsy Sun Wukong Sandy Xuanzang	Bai Tao Zhao Guohua Zhu Zhongyong Miao Bin	1992
4.25	Peking	*Monkey and the Cave of Spiders*	Shanghai Beijing Opera Theatre	Sun Wukong Replicas	Unknown	1992
5.1	Cantonese	*Reunion in the Moon Palace*	Chung Sun Sing Cantonese Opera Troupe	Yang Guifei Emperor Ming	Chen Hou-Keo Lam Kar-Sing	1993
5.2	Peking	*The Intoxicated Concubine*	Liaoling Youth Beijing Opera Troupe	Eunuch Gao Yang Guifei	Chang Jing Liu Yajun	1986
5.3	Anhui	*The Intoxicated Concubine*	Anhui Provincial Hui Opera Troupe	Yang Guifei	Luo Liping	1991

Photo	Genre	Opera	Troupe	Characters	Performers	Year
5.4	Cantonese	*The Emperor's Daughter*	Yeung Ming Cantonese Opera Troupe	Zhou Shixian Princess Changping	Lau Wai-Ming Chan Wing-Yee	1995
5.5	Cantonese	*The Emperor's Daughter*	Zhuhai Cantonese Opera Troupe	Princess Changping Zhou Shixian	Bai Xuehong Yao Zhiqiang	1993
5.6	Cantonese	*The Emperor's Daughter*	Zhuhai Cantonese Opera Troupe	Princess Changping Zhou Shixian	Bai Xuehong Yao Zhiqiang	1993
5.7	Cantonese	*The Emperor's Daughter*	Yeung Ming Cantonese Opera Troupe	Princess Changping Zhou Shixian	Chan Wing-Yee Lau Wai-Ming	1995
5.8	Yue	'In the Emperor's Garden'	Red Mansion Opera Troupe of Shanghai Shaoxing Opera Theatre	Emperor Meng Lijun	Xu Yulan Wang Wenjuan	1991
5.9	Yue	'In the Emperor's Garden'	Red Mansion Opera Troupe of Shanghai Shaoxing Opera Theatre	Meng Lijun Emperor	Wang Wenjuan Xu Yulan	1991
5.10	Sichuan	'Wresting the Dragon Throne'	Chengdu Sichuan Opera Theatre No. 3 Company	Yang Guang	Xiao Ting	1991
5.11	Sichuan	'Wresting the Dragon Throne'	Chengdu Sichuan Opera Theatre No. 3 Company	Yang Guang	Xiao Ting	1991
5.12	Sichuan	'Wresting the Dragon Throne'	Chengdu Sichuan Opera Theatre No. 3 Company	Empress Yang Guang	Liu Keli Xiao Ting	1991
5.13	Jin	*Death in the Palace*	Shanxi Provincial Jin Opera Troupe	Su Yu'e Emperor Yin Liu Guilian	Chang Xiangguo Gao Yalin Mi Xiaomin	1986
5.14	Jin	*Death in the Palace*	Shanxi Provincial Jin Opera Troupe	Emperor Yin Liu Guilian Su Yu'e	Gao Yalin Mi Xiaomin Chang Xiangguo	1986
5.15	Jin	*Death in the Palace*	Shanxi Provincial Jin Opera Troupe	Liu Guilian Su Yu'e	Mi Xiaomin Chang Xiangguo	1986
5.16	Cantonese	*The Emperor and the Concubine*	Foshan Cantonese Opera Troupe	Wu Yunzhu Emperor Shunzhi	Cao Xiuqin Peng Chiquan	1991
5.17	Cantonese	*The Emperor and the Concubine*	Foshan Cantonese Opera Troupe	Emperor Shunzhi Wu Yunzhu	Peng Chiquan Cao Xiuqin	1991
5.18	Cantonese	*The Emperor and the Concubine*	Foshan Cantonese Opera Troupe	Emperor Shunzhi	Peng Chiquan	1991
6.1	Peking	*An Auspicious Marriage*	Peking Opera Performing Artists Troupe of China	Zhou Yu	Song Xiaochuan	1985
6.2	Peking	*The Changban Slopes*	Peking Opera Performing Artists Troupe of China	Zhao Yun	Li Huiliang	1985
6.3	Peking	*The Changban Slopes*	Peking Opera Performing Artists Troupe of China	Zhang Fei	Zhang Nianxiang	1985
6.4	Peking	*Summoning the East Wind*	Peking Opera Performing Artists Troupe of China	Zhuge Liang	Zhang Xuejin	1985
6.5	Peking	*The Huarong Pass*	Peking Opera Performing Artists Troupe of China	Guan Yu	Li Huiliang	1985
6.6	Peking	*The Huarong Pass*	Peking Opera Performing Artists Troupe of China	Cao Cao	Yuan Shihai	1985
6.7	Anhui	*Meeting at the Riverbank*	Anhui Provincial Hui Opera Troupe	Zhou Yu	Li Longbin	1991
6.8	Peking	*Memorial to a Rival*	Shanghai Beijing Opera Theatre	Zhuge Liang	Yan Xingpeng	1992
6.9	Peking	*Cao Cao and Yang Xiu*	Shanghai Beijing Opera Theatre	Cao Cao Gongsun Han Kong Wendai	Shang Changrong Sheng Xiechang Li Dacheng	1992

Photo	Genre	Opera	Troupe	Characters	Performers	Year
6.10	Peking	*Cao Cao and Yang Xiu*	Shanghai Beijing Opera Theatre	Yang Xiu	Yan Xingpeng	1992
6.11	Peking	*Cao Cao and Yang Xiu*	Shanghai Beijing Opera Theatre	Cao Cao Yang Xiu Cao Hong	Shang Changrong Yan Xingpeng Zhu Zhongyong	1992
6.12	Hebei Clapper	*Burning the Camps*	Hebei Clapper Opera Troupe	Liu Bei	Pei Yanling	1991
6.13	Hebei Clapper	*Burning the Camps*	Hebei Clapper Opera Troupe	Zhao Yun	Pei Yanling	1991
6.14	Jiangxi	*Yang Paifeng Accepts a Challenge*	Jiangxi Gan Opera Troupe	Yang Paifeng Meng Liang	Tu Linghui Li Weide	1992
6.15	Jiangxi	*Yang Paifeng Accepts a Challenge*	Jiangxi Gan Opera Troupe	Meng Liang Yang Paifeng	Li Weide Tu Linghui	1992
6.16	Jiangxi	*Yang Paifeng Accepts a Challenge*	Jiangxi Gan Opera Troupe	Yang Paifeng	Tu Linghui	1992
6.17	Peking	*The Warrior Maiden Mu Guiying*	Liaoling Youth Beijing Opera Troupe	Mu Guiying Yang Zongbao	Wang Yulan An Yi	1986
6.18	Peking	*The Warrior Maiden Mu Guiying*	Liaoling Youth Beijing Opera Troupe	Mu Guiying	Wang Yulan	1986
6.19	Peking	*The Warrior Maiden Mu Guiying*	Liaoling Youth Beijing Opera Troupe	Yang Zongbao	An Yi	1986
6.20	Longjiang	*Twice-Locked Mountain*	Heilongjiang Provincial Longjiang Opera Experimental Theatre	Liu Jinding	Bai Shuxian	1991
6.21	Longjiang	*Twice-Locked Mountain*	Heilongjiang Provincial Longjiang Opera Experimental Theatre	Liu Jinding Gao Junbao	Bai Shuxian Sun Chunqiu	1991
6.22	Longjiang	*Twice-Locked Mountain*	Heilongjiang Provincial Longjiang Opera Experimental Theatre	Liu Jinding	Bai Shuxian	1991
6.23	Peking	*Princess Baihua*	Shanghai Beijing Opera Theatre	Hai Jun Jiang Huayou Princess Baihua	Wang Shimin Zhu Juli Zhang Nanyun	1992
6.24	Anhui	*Princess Baihua*	Anhui Provincial Hui Opera Troupe	Princess Baihua	Zhang Min	1991
6.25	Hebei Clapper	*Death at Prayer*	Hebei Clapper Opera Troupe	Lady Nanning Wu Han	Zhang Qiuling Liu Fengling	1992
6.26	Hebei Clapper	*Death at Prayer*	Hebei Clapper Opera Troupe	Wu Han Lady Nanning	Liu Fengling Zhang Qiuling	1992
6.27	Hebei Clapper	*Prince Lanling*	Hebei Clapper Opera Troupe	Prince Lanling	Pei Yanling	1992
6.28	Hebei Clapper	*Prince Lanling*	Hebei Clapper Opera Troupe	Prince Lanling	Pei Yanling	1992
6.29	Hebei Clapper	*Prince Lanling*	Hebei Clapper Opera Troupe	Prince Lanling	Pei Yanling	1992
7.1	Yue	*The Poet Divorces His Wife*	Zhejiang Little Flowers Shaoxing Opera Troupe	Lu You	Mao Weitao	1990
7.2	Yue	*Judge Bao's Apology*	Zhejiang Little Flowers Shaoxing Opera Troupe	Bao Zheng	Dong Kedi	1991
7.3	Yue	*Judge Bao's Apology*	Zhejiang Little Flowers Shaoxing Opera Troupe	Bao Zheng Wang Fengying	Dong Kedi Hong Ying	1991
7.4	Shaoxing	*The Prime Minister of Wei*	Zhejiang Provincial Shaoxing Shao Opera Troupe	Zhai Huang	Zhou Jianying	1991
7.5	Shaoxing	*The Prime Minister of Wei*	Zhejiang Provincial Shaoxing Shao Opera Troupe	Yue Yang	Hu Jianxin	1991
7.6	Shaoxing	*The Prime Minister of Wei*	Zhejiang Provincial Shaoxing Shao Opera Troupe	Zhai Huang	Zhong Guoliang	1991
7.7	Cantonese	*Jing Ke, the Loyal Assassin*	Ming Chi Shing Cantonese Opera Troupe	Crown Princess Prince of Yan	Wan Fei-Yin Koi Ming-Fai	1992

Photo	Genre	Opera	Troupe	Characters	Performers	Year
7.8	Cantonese	*Jing Ke, the Loyal Assassin*	Ming Chi Shing Cantonese Opera Troupe	Jing Ke King of Qin	Luo Pinchao Yau Sing-Po	1992
7.9	Cantonese	*Jing Ke, the Loyal Assassin*	Ming Chi Shing Cantonese Opera Troupe	King of Qin Jing Ke	Yau Sing-Po Luo Pinchao	1992
7.10	Cantonese	*Jing Ke, the Loyal Assassin*	Ming Chi Shing Cantonese Opera Troupe	Jing Ke	Luo Pinchao	1992
7.11	Yue	*The Ode to Constancy*	Zhejiang Little Flowers Shaoxing Opera Troupe	Zhuo Wenjun	He Saifei	1991
7.12	Yue	*The Ode to Constancy*	Zhejiang Little Flowers Shaoxing Opera Troupe	Zhuo Wenjun Sima Xiangru	He Saifei Xia Saili	1991
7.13	Yue	*The Ode to Constancy*	Zhejiang Little Flowers Shaoxing Opera Troupe	Zhuo Wenjun Sima Xiangru	He Saifei Xia Saili	1991
7.14	Ping	'Death in the Temple'	Hebei Shijiazhuang Youth Ping Opera Troupe	Han Qi Dong Ge Chun Mei	Yang Chunli Guo Jinxia Zhang Yanhong	1991
7.15	Ping	'Death in the Temple'	Hebei Shijiazhuang Youth Ping Opera Troupe	Qin Xianglian Han Qi	Wang Jing Yang Chunli	1991
7.16	Yue	*Chen Sanliang* *(Virtue amid the Flowers)*	Zhejiang Little Flowers Shaoxing Opera Troupe	Li Suping	Huang Yiqun	1990
7.17	Yue	*Virtue amid the Flowers*	Shanghai Shaoxing Opera Theatre No. 3 Company	Li Suping	Lü Ruiying	1988
7.18	Yue	*Chen Sanliang* *(Virtue amid the Flowers)*	Zhejiang Little Flowers Shaoxing Opera Troupe	Li Suping Li Fengming	Huang Yiqun Shao Yan	1990
8.1	Yue	*The Scenic Garden* *(Dream of the Red Chamber)*	Zhejiang Little Flowers Shaoxing Opera Troupe	Jia Yuanchun	Ying Huizhu	1986
8.2	Yue	*Daughters*	Zhejiang Little Flowers Shaoxing Opera Troupe	Cuiyun Third daughter Third son-in-law	He Saifei Ying Huizhu Fang Xuewen	1990
8.3	Yue	*Daughters*	Zhejiang Little Flowers Shaoxing Opera Troupe	Cuiyun Zou Shilong	He Saifei Mao Weitao	1990
8.4	Yue	*Daughters*	Zhejiang Little Flowers Shaoxing Opera Troupe	Lady Yang Yang Jikang	Xu Aiwu Dong Kedi	1990
8.5	Yue	*The Scenic Garden* *(Dream of the Red Chamber)*	Zhejiang Little Flowers Shaoxing Opera Troupe	Jia Baoyu	Mao Weitao	1986
8.6	Huangmei	*Dream of the Red Chamber*	Anhui Provincial Huangmei Opera Theatre	Lin Daiyu Jia Baoyu	Wu Yaling Ma Lan	1993
8.7	Yue	*The Scenic Garden* *(Dream of the Red Chamber)*	Zhejiang Little Flowers Shaoxing Opera Troupe	Xue Baochai	He Ying	1986
8.8	Yue	*The Scenic Garden* *(Dream of the Red Chamber)*	Zhejiang Little Flowers Shaoxing Opera Troupe	Lin Daiyu	He Saifei	1986
8.9	Huangmei	*Dream of the Red Chamber*	Anhui Provincial Huangmei Opera Theatre	Lin Daiyu Jia Baoyu	Wu Yaling Ma Lan	1993
8.10	Cantonese	*Why Won't You Return?*	Sun Ma Cantonese Opera Troupe	Lady Wen Wen Pingsheng Zhao Pinniang	Wen Juefei Sun Ma Sze-Tsang Zeng Hui	1984
8.11	Cantonese	*Why Won't You Return?*	Sun Ma Cantonese Opera Troupe	Wen Pingsheng	Sun Ma Sze-Tsang	1984

Photo	Genre	Opera	Troupe	Characters	Performers	Year
8.12	Cantonese	*The Purple Hairpin*	Chor Fung Ming Cantonese Opera Troupe	Huo Xiaoyu Li Yi	Mui Suet-See Lung Kim-Sang	1984
8.13	Cantonese	*The Purple Hairpin*	Chor Fung Ming Cantonese Opera Troupe	Huo Xiaoyu	Mui Suet-See	1984
8.14	Cantonese	*The Purple Hairpin*	Chor Fung Ming Cantonese Opera Troupe	The Man in Yellow Huo Xiaoyu Huansha	Chu Sau-Ying Mui Suet-See Yum Bing-Yee	1984
8.15	Sichuan	*Pi Jin Plays the Fool*	Chengdu Hibiscus Sichuan Opera Troupe	Pi Jin's wife Pi Jin	Xiao Daifen Su Mingde	1988
8.16	Sichuan	*Pi Jin Plays the Fool*	Chengdu Hibiscus Sichuan Opera Troupe	Pi Jin	Su Mingde	1988
8.17	Yue	*The Romance of the West Chamber*	Zhejiang Little Flowers Shaoxing Opera Troupe	Cui Yingying Zhang Junrui	Tao Huimin Mao Weitao	1991
8.18	Yue	*The Romance of the West Chamber*	Zhejiang Little Flowers Shaoxing Opera Troupe	Zhang Junrui	Mao Weitao	1991
8.19	Yue	*The Romance of the West Chamber*	Zhejiang Little Flowers Shaoxing Opera Troupe	Cui Yingying	Tao Huimin	1991
8.20	Yue	*The Romance of the West Chamber*	Zhejiang Little Flowers Shaoxing Opera Troupe	Cui Yingying Zhang Junrui	Tao Huimin Mao Weitao	1991
9.1	Qin	*Slay the Dog*	Shaanxi Youth Qin Opera Troupe	Madam Jiao Cao Zhuang	Xiao Ying Li Xiaofeng	1990
9.2	Ping	*The Jade Bracelet*	Hebei Shijiazhuang Youth Ping Opera Troupe	Sun Yujiao	Liu Fengzhi	1991
9.3	Cantonese	*The Jade Bracelet*	Tuen Mun Cantonese Opera Troupe	Sun Yujiao	Chan Sau-Hing	1981
9.4	Ping	*The Jade Bracelet*	Hebei Shijiazhuang Youth Ping Opera Troupe	Sun Yujiao Mother Liu	Liu Fengzhi Jin Lingzhan	1991
9.5	Ping	*Liu Ling Gets Drunk*	Hebei Shijiazhuang Youth Ping Opera Troupe	Liu Ling	Zhao Lihua	1991
9.6	Ping	*Liu Ling Gets Drunk*	Hebei Shijiazhuang Youth Ping Opera Troupe	Liu Ling Du Kang	Zhao Lihua Yang Chunli	1991
9.7	Ping	*Liu Ling Gets Drunk*	Hebei Shijiazhuang Youth Ping Opera Troupe	Liu Ling Du Kang	Zhao Lihua Yang Chunli	1991
9.8	Chaozhou	*A Gift of Wine*	Guangdong Chaozhou Opera Troupe	Doorkeeper	Ke Lizheng	1984
9.9	Chaozhou	*A Gift of Wine*	Guangdong Chaozhou Opera Troupe	Doorkeeper Wang Maosheng	Ke Lizheng Chen Qinmeng	1984
9.10	Chaozhou	*A Gift of Wine*	Guangdong Chaozhou Opera Troupe	Wang Maosheng Xue Rengui Doorkeeper	Chen Qinmeng Chen Guangyao Ke Lizheng	1984
9.11	Jiangxi	*The Story of Dou E*	Jiangxi Gan Opera Troupe	Dou E Widow Cai	Tu Linghui Xiong Liyun	1992
9.12	Jiangxi	*The Story of Dou E*	Jiangxi Gan Opera Troupe	Dou E	Tu Linghui	1992
9.13	Jiangxi	*The Story of Dou E*	Jiangxi Gan Opera Troupe	Dou E Dou Tianzhang	Tu Linghui Li Weide	1992
9.14	Jiangxi	'Dream of the Coronet and the Belt'	Jiangxi Gan Opera Troupe	Cui	Tu Linghui	1992
9.15	Jiangxi	'Dream of the Coronet and the Belt'	Jiangxi Gan Opera Troupe	Cui	Tu Linghui	1992

Photo	Genre	Opera	Troupe	Characters	Performers	Year
9.16	Jiangxi	'Dream of the Coronet and the Belt'	Jiangxi Gan Opera Troupe	Cui	Tu Linghui	1992
9.17	Jin	*Third Wife Teaches Her Son*	Shanxi Provincial Jin Opera Troupe	Xue Bao, servant Xue Yingge, son Wang Chun'e	Zhao Xiaolei Li Yunli Li Guilian	1986
9.18	Jin	*Third Wife Teaches Her Son*	Shanxi Provincial Jin Opera Troupe	Xue Yingge, son Wang Chun'e	Li Yunli Li Guilian	1986
10.1	Sichuan	*The Legend of the White Snake*	Chengdu Sichuan Opera Theatre No. 3 Company	Fahai	Sun Puxie	1991
10.2	Peking	*The Thirsty Monk*	Liaoling Youth Beijing Opera Troupe	Wine seller Lu Zhishen	Li Xiaoliang Zhao Hui	1986
10.3	Peking	*The Thirsty Monk*	Liaoling Youth Beijing Opera Troupe	Lu Zhishen Wine seller	Zhao Hui Li Xiaoliang	1986
10.4	Peking	*The Thirsty Monk*	Liaoling Youth Beijing Opera Troupe	Lu Zhishen Wine seller	Zhao Hui Li Xiaoliang	1986
10.5	Anhui	*Two Flee Religious Life*	Anhui Provincial Hui Opera Troupe	Wuming	Zhang Min	1991
10.6	Anhui	*Two Flee Religious Life*	Anhui Provincial Hui Opera Troupe	Benwu Wuming	Xu Yousheng Zhang Min	1991
10.7	Yue	*Two Flee Religious Life*	Ningshao Little Flowers Shaoxing Opera Troupe	Wuming Benwu	Zhou Shujun Pan Qin	1990
10.8	Yue	*Finding Mother in a Convent*	The Red Mansion Opera Troupe of the Shanghai Shaoxing Opera Theatre	Zhizhen	Jin Caifeng	1991
10.9	Yue	*Finding Mother in a Convent*	The Red Mansion Opera Troupe of the Shanghai Shaoxing Opera Theatre	Zhizhen Xu Yuanzai	Jin Caifeng Qian Huili	1991
11.1	Hebei Clapper	*Wu Song's Revenge*	Hebei Clapper Opera Troupe	Wu Song	Pei Yanling	1992
11.2	Hebei Clapper	*Night Flight*	Hebei Clapper Opera Troupe	Lin Chong	Pei Yanling	1992
11.3	Peking	*Li Kui Visits His Mother*	Shanghai Beijing Opera Theatre	Li Kui	Shang Changrong	1992
11.4	Peking	*Li Kui Visits His Mother*	Shenyang Beijing Opera Theatre	Li's mother Li Kui	Xu Jun Wang Qingyuan	1992
11.5	Hebei Clapper	*Wu Song's Revenge*	Hebei Clapper Opera Troupe	Wu Song	Pei Yanling	1992
11.6	Hebei Clapper	*Wu Song's Revenge*	Hebei Clapper Opera Troupe	Wu Song	Pei Yanling	1991
11.7	Hebei Clapper	*Wu Song's Revenge*	Hebei Clapper Opera Troupe	Jiang the Gate God Wu Song	Sun Fentian Pei Yanling	1991
11.8	Hebei Clapper	*Wu Song's Revenge*	Hebei Clapper Opera Troupe	Wu Song	Pei Yanling	1992
11.9	Hebei Clapper	*Wu Song's Revenge*	Hebei Clapper Opera Troupe	Wu Song	Pei Yanling	1992
12.1	Qin	*Sorrow at West Lake (Red Plum Blossoms)*	Shaanxi Youth Qin Opera Troupe	Li Huiniang	Li Mei	1990
12.2	Hebei Clapper	*Zhong Kui Arranges a Marriage*	Hebei Clapper Opera Troupe	Zhong Kui Yang Guosong, the chief examiner	Pei Yanling Zhang Fengshan	1991
12.3	Hebei Clapper	*Zhong Kui Arranges a Marriage*	Hebei Clapper Opera Troupe	Zhong Kui	Pei Yanling	1991
12.4	Hebei Clapper	*Zhong Kui Arranges a Marriage*	Hebei Clapper Opera Troupe	Zhong Kui	Pei Yanling	1991

Photo	Genre	Opera	Troupe	Characters	Performers	Year
12.5	Hebei Clapper	*Zhong Kui Arranges a Marriage*	Hebei Clapper Opera Troupe	Zhong Kui	Pei Yanling	1991
12.6	Hebei Clapper	*Zhong Kui Arranges a Marriage*	Hebei Clapper Opera Troupe	Zhong Kui Zhong Meiying	Pei Yanling Peng Huiheng	1991
12.7	Sichuan	*The Haunting of Zhang Sanlang*	Chengdu Sichuan Opera Theatre No. 3 Company	Yan Xijiao Zhang Sanlang	Tian Huiwen Li Zenglin	1991
12.8	Sichuan	*The Haunting of Zhang Sanlang*	Chengdu Sichuan Opera Theatre No. 3 Company	Zhang Sanlang	Li Zenglin	1991
12.9	Sichuan	*The Haunting of Zhang Sanlang*	Chengdu Sichuan Opera Theatre No. 3 Company	Yan Xijiao Zhang Sanlang	Tian Huiwen Li Zenglin	1991
12.10	Cantonese	*Red Plum Blossoms*	Zhuhai Cantonese Opera Troupe	Pei Yu	Yao Zhiqiang	1993
12.11	Cantonese	*Red Plum Blossoms*	Zhuhai Cantonese Opera Troupe	Lu Zhaorong Jia Sidao	Bai Xuehong Guan Yaotang	1993
12.12	Qin	*Sorrow at West Lake (Red Plum Blossoms)*	Shaanxi Youth Qin Opera Troupe	Li Huiniang Pei Yu	Xiao Ying Li Xiaofeng	1990
12.13	Qin	*Sorrow at West Lake (Red Plum Blossoms)*	Shaanxi Youth Qin Opera Troupe	Li Huiniang	Xiao Ying	1990
12.14	Sichuan	*The Wrath of the Fox Fairy*	Chengdu Sichuan Opera Theatre No. 3 Company	Shi Huaiyu	Sun Yongbo	1991
12.15	Sichuan	*The Wrath of the Fox Fairy*	Chengdu Sichuan Opera Theatre No. 3 Company	Fox Fairy Shi Huaiyu	Chen Qiaoru Sun Yongbo	1991
12.16	Sichuan	*The Wrath of the Fox Fairy*	Chengdu Sichuan Opera Theatre No. 3 Company	Shi Huaiyu Fox Fairy	Sun Yongbo Chen Qiaoru	1991
12.17	Cantonese	*The Peony Pavilion*	Chor Fung Ming Cantonese Opera Troupe	Chunxiang Du Liniang	Yum Bing-Yee Mui Suet-See	1984
12.18	Cantonese	*The Peony Pavilion*	Chor Fung Ming Cantonese Opera Troupe	Liu Mengmei Du Liniang	Lung Kim-Sang Mui Suet-See	1984
12.19	Cantonese	*The Peony Pavilion*	Chor Fung Ming Cantonese Opera Troupe	Liu Mengmei	Lung Kim-Sang	1984
12.20	Chaozhou	*A Woodshed Encounter*	Guangdong Chaozhou Opera Troupe	Mo Erniang Li Laosan	Wu Ling'er Fang Zhanrong	1991
12.21	Chaozhou	*A Woodshed Encounter*	Guangdong Chaozhou Opera Troupe	Li Laosan	Fang Zhanrong	1991
13.1	Peking	*The Young Widow at the Grave*	Liaoling Youth Beijing Opera Troupe	Liu Jinglu Xiao Suzhen	Li Xiaoliang Guan Bo	1986

Note: In this table, only the main performers or characters in the photographs are identified, from left to right or from top to bottom.

Appendix B: Chinese Guide to Photographs

照片	劇 種	劇 目	劇 團	劇中人	扮演人	年份
p. ii	川	人間好	成都市芙蓉花川劇團	白鱔仙姑	喻海燕	1988
1.1	龍江	皇親國戚	黑龍江省龍江劇實驗劇院	白忙 沈夢得 夫人 衛高	李瑞剛 高雲程 呂冬梅 趙友山	1991
3.5	京	秦香蓮	天津市青年京劇團	秦香蓮	雷英	1987
3.6	越	雙珠鳳	浙江小百花越劇團	霍定金	何賽飛	1990
3.7	京	小上墳	遼寧青少年京劇團	蕭素貞	管波	1986
3.8	贛	拒詔撲火	江西省贛劇團	介之推 介母	李維德 陳肖霞	1992
3.9	京	虹橋贈珠	瀋陽京劇院	凌波仙子	李靜文	1993
3.10	贛	選馬出征	江西省贛劇團	穆桂英	陳俐	1992
3.11	越	雙珠鳳	浙江小百花越劇團	文必正	夏賽麗	1990
3.12	粵	牡丹亭驚夢	雛鳳鳴粵劇團	杜寶	靚次伯	1985
3.13	昆	雅觀樓	中國昆劇藝術團	李存孝	王芝泉	1989
3.14	京	長坂坡	天津市青年京劇團	趙雲	王立軍	1987
3.15	京	秦香蓮	天津市青年京劇團	包拯	孟廣祿	1987
3.16	川	皮金滾燈	成都市芙蓉花川劇團	皮金	蘇明德	1988
3.17	越	何文秀	浙江小百花越劇團	楊媽媽	俞會珍	1990
4.1	川	白蛇傳	成都市芙蓉花川劇團	火神 韋馱 鐃鉢 哼哈二將	不詳	1988
4.2	川	芙蓉花仙	成都市芙蓉花川劇團	芙蓉花仙	喻海燕	1988
4.3	川	芙蓉花仙	成都市芙蓉花川劇團	芙蓉花仙	喻海燕	1988
4.4	川	芙蓉花仙	成都市芙蓉花川劇團	芙蓉花仙 陳秋林	喻海燕 陳智林	1988
4.5	川	芙蓉花仙	成都市芙蓉花川劇團	芭蕉精	楊永捷	1988
4.6	川	白蛇傳	成都市川劇院三團	青蛇 白蛇	劉萍 陳巧茹	1991
4.7	川	白蛇傳	成都市芙蓉花川劇團	白蛇 青蛇	李莎 涂鐵軍	1988

照片	劇種	劇目	劇團	劇中人	扮演人	年份
4.8	川	白蛇傳	成都市川劇院三團	許仙 法海 白蛇 青蛇 王道陵	孫湧波 孫普協 陳巧茹 朱建國 李增林	1991
4.9	川	白蛇傳	成都市川劇院三團	鐃缽	曉艇	1991
4.10	徽	斷橋	安徽省徽劇團	白蛇 許仙 青蛇	羅麗萍 李泰山 賈憶萍	1991
4.11	潮	斷橋會	廣東潮劇團	白蛇 許仙	曾馥 鍾怡坤	1984
4.12	京	八仙過海	遼寧青少年京劇團	鍾離權 藍采和 何仙姑 李鐵拐 張果老 曹國舅	馬正光 張威 王玉蘭 姜大光 常兢 羅怡春	1986
4.13	京	八仙過海	遼寧青少年京劇團	金魚仙子	薛俊秋	1986
4.14	京	八仙過海	遼寧青少年京劇團	金魚仙子	薛俊秋	1986
4.15	京	八仙過海	遼寧青少年京劇團	呂洞賓 金魚仙子	吳坤 薛俊秋	1986
4.16	徽	戲牡丹	安徽省徽劇團	呂洞賓	曹尚禮	1991
4.17	徽	戲牡丹	安徽省徽劇團	白牡丹	李小紅	1991
4.18	河北梆子	鬧天宮	河北梆子戲劇團	孫悟空	裴艷玲	1992
4.19	京	鬧天宮	天津市青年京劇團	巨靈神 孫悟空	陳璽強 石曉亮	1990
4.20	紹	三借芭蕉扇	浙江紹興紹劇團	孫悟空 豬八戒	劉建揚 七小齡童	1991
4.21	紹	三借芭蕉扇	浙江紹興紹劇團	孫悟空	劉建揚	1991
4.22	紹	三打白骨精	浙江紹興紹劇團	白骨精	孫曉燕	1991
4.23	紹	三打白骨精	浙江紹興紹劇團	玄奘 老人	王振芳 鍾國良	1991
4.24	京	盤絲洞	上海京劇院	豬八戒 孫悟空 沙僧 玄奘	白濤 趙國華 朱忠勇 繆斌	1992
4.25	京	盤絲洞	上海京劇院	孫悟空 化身	不詳	1992
5.1	粵	唐明皇會太真	頌新聲劇團	楊貴妃 唐明皇	陳好逑 林家聲	1993
5.2	京	貴妃醉酒	遼寧青少年京劇團	高力士 楊貴妃	常兢 劉亞君	1986
5.3	徽	貴妃醉酒	安徽省徽劇團	楊貴妃	羅麗萍	1991

照片	劇種	劇目	劇團	劇中人	扮演人	年份
5.4	粵	帝女花	揚鳴粵劇團	周世顯 長平公主	劉惠鳴 陳詠儀	1995
5.5	粵	帝女花	珠海市粵劇團	長平公主 周世顯	白雪紅 姚志強	1993
5.6	粵	帝女花	珠海市粵劇團	長平公主 周世顯	白雪紅 姚志強	1993
5.7	粵	帝女花	揚鳴粵劇團	長平公主 周世顯	陳詠儀 劉惠鳴	1995
5.8	越	游上林	上海越劇院紅樓劇團	皇帝 孟麗君	徐玉蘭 王文娟	1991
5.9	越	游上林	上海越劇院紅樓劇團	孟麗君 皇帝	王文娟 徐玉蘭	1991
5.10	川	問病逼宮	成都市川劇院三團	楊廣	曉艇	1991
5.11	川	問病逼宮	成都市川劇院三團	楊廣	曉艇	1991
5.12	川	問病逼宮	成都市川劇院三團	國太 楊廣	劉克莉 曉艇	1991
5.13	晉	殺宮	山西省晉劇團	蘇玉娥 漢隱帝 劉桂蓮	常香果 高亞林 米曉敏	1986
5.14	晉	殺宮	山西省晉劇團	漢隱帝 劉桂蓮 蘇玉娥	高亞林 米曉敏 常香果	1986
5.15	晉	殺宮	山西省晉劇團	劉桂蓮 蘇玉娥	米曉敏 常香果	1986
5.16	粵	順治與董鄂妃	佛山粵劇團	烏雲珠 順治帝	曹秀琴 彭熾權	1991
5.17	粵	順治與董鄂妃	佛山粵劇團	順治帝 烏雲珠	彭熾權 曹秀琴	1991
5.18	粵	順治與董鄂妃	佛山粵劇團	順治帝	彭熾權	1991
6.1	京	龍鳳呈祥	中國京劇藝術家演出團	周瑜	宋小川	1985
6.2	京	長坂坡	中國京劇藝術家演出團	趙雲	厲慧良	1985
6.3	京	長坂坡	中國京劇藝術家演出團	張飛	張年祥	1985
6.4	京	借東風	中國京劇藝術家演出團	諸葛亮	張學津	1985
6.5	京	華容道	中國京劇藝術家演出團	關羽	厲慧良	1985
6.6	京	華容道	中國京劇藝術家演出團	曹操	袁世海	1985
6.7	徽	臨江會	安徽省徽劇團	周瑜	李龍斌	1991
6.8	京	臥龍吊孝	上海京劇院	諸葛亮	言興朋	1992
6.9	京	曹操與楊修	上海京劇院	曹操 公孫涵 孔文岱	尚長榮 盛變昌 李達成	1992

照片	劇種	劇目	劇團	劇中人	扮演人	年份
6.10	京	曹操與楊修	上海京劇院	楊修	言興朋	1992
6.11	京	曹操與楊修	上海京劇院	曹操 楊修 曹洪	尚長榮 言興朋 朱忠勇	1992
6.12	河北梆子	火燒連營	河北梆子戲劇團	劉備	裴豔玲	1991
6.13	河北梆子	火燒連營	河北梆子戲劇團	趙雲	裴豔玲	1991
6.14	贛	孟良搬兵	江西省贛劇團	楊排風 孟良	涂玲慧 李維德	1992
6.15	贛	孟良搬兵	江西省贛劇團	孟良 楊排風	李維德 涂玲慧	1992
6.16	贛	孟良搬兵	江西省贛劇團	楊排風	涂玲慧	1992
6.17	京	穆桂英下山破陣	遼寧青少年京劇團	穆桂英 楊宗保	王玉蘭 安怡	1986
6.18	京	穆桂英下山破陣	遼寧青少年京劇團	穆桂英	王玉蘭	1986
6.19	京	穆桂英下山破陣	遼寧青少年京劇團	楊宗保	安怡	1986
6.20	龍江	雙鎖山	黑龍江省龍江劇實驗劇院	劉金定	白淑賢	1991
6.21	龍江	雙鎖山	黑龍江省龍江劇實驗劇院	劉金定 高君保	白淑賢 孫春秋	1991
6.22	龍江	雙鎖山	黑龍江省龍江劇實驗劇院	劉金定	白淑賢	1991
6.23	京	百花公主	上海京劇院	海俊 江花佑 百花公主	王世民 朱菊麗 張南雲	1992
6.24	徽	哭劍飲恨	安徽省徽劇團	百花公主	張敏	1991
6.25	河北梆子	吳漢殺妻	河北梆子戲劇團	南寧公主 吳漢	張秋玲 劉鳳嶺	1992
6.26	河北梆子	吳漢殺妻	河北梆子戲劇團	吳漢 南寧公主	劉鳳嶺 張秋玲	1992
6.27	河北梆子	蘭陵王	河北梆子戲劇團	蘭陵王	裴艷玲	1992
6.28	河北梆子	蘭陵王	河北梆子戲劇團	蘭陵王	裴艷玲	1992
6.29	河北梆子	蘭陵王	河北梆子戲劇團	蘭陵王	裴艷玲	1992
7.1	越	陸游與唐婉	浙江小百花越劇團	陸游	茅威濤	1990
7.2	越	包公賠情	浙江小百花越劇團	包拯	董柯娣	1991
7.3	越	包公賠情	浙江小百花越劇團	包拯 王鳳英	董柯娣 洪瑛	1991
7.4	紹	相國志	浙江紹興紹劇團	翟璜	周劍英	1991
7.5	紹	相國志	浙江紹興紹劇團	樂羊	胡建新	1991
7.6	紹	相國志	浙江紹興紹劇團	翟璜	鍾國良	1991
7.7	粵	荊軻	鳴芝聲劇團	儲妃 燕太子	尹飛燕 蓋鳴輝	1992

照片	劇 種	劇 目	劇 團	劇中人	扮演人	年份
7.8	粵	荊軻	鳴芝聲劇團	荊軻 秦王	羅品超 尤聲普	1992
7.9	粵	荊軻	鳴芝聲劇團	秦王 荊軻	尤聲普 羅品超	1992
7.10	粵	荊軻	鳴芝聲劇團	荊軻	羅品超	1992
7.11	越	白頭吟	浙江小百花越劇團	卓文君	何賽飛	1991
7.12	越	白頭吟	浙江小百花越劇團	卓文君 司馬相如	何賽飛 夏賽麗	1991
7.13	越	白頭吟	浙江小百花越劇團	卓文君 司馬相如	何賽飛 夏賽麗	1991
7.14	評	殺廟	河北石家莊青年評劇團	韓琪 冬哥 春妹	楊春利 國金霞 張艷紅	1991
7.15	評	殺廟	河北石家莊青年評劇團	秦香蓮 韓琪	王靜 楊春利	1991
7.16	越	陳三兩	浙江小百花越劇團	李素萍	黃依群	1990
7.17	越	花中君子	上海越劇院三團	李素萍	呂瑞英	1988
7.18	越	陳三兩	浙江小百花越劇團	李素萍 李鳳鳴	黃依群 邵雁	1990
8.1	越	大觀園	浙江小百花越劇團	賈元春	應惠珠	1986
8.2	越	五女拜壽	浙江小百花越劇團	翠雲 三女兒 三女婿	何賽飛 應惠珠 方雪雯	1990
8.3	越	五女拜壽	浙江小百花越劇團	翠雲 鄒仕龍	何賽飛 茅威濤	1990
8.4	越	五女拜壽	浙江小百花越劇團	楊夫人 楊繼康	徐愛武 董柯娣	1990
8.5	越	大觀園	浙江小百花越劇團	賈寶玉	茅威濤	1986
8.6	黃梅	紅樓夢	安徽省黃梅戲劇院	林黛玉 賈寶玉	吳亞玲 馬蘭	1993
8.7	越	大觀園	浙江小百花越劇團	薛寶釵	何英	1986
8.8	越	大觀園	浙江小百花越劇團	林黛玉	何賽飛	1986
8.9	黃梅	紅樓夢	安徽省黃梅戲劇院	林黛玉 賈寶玉	吳亞玲 馬蘭	1993
8.10	粵	胡不歸	新馬劇團	文夫人 文萍生 趙顰娘	文覺非 新馬師曾 曾慧	1984
8.11	粵	胡不歸	新馬劇團	文萍生	新馬師曾	1984

照片	劇種	劇目	劇團	劇中人	扮演人	年份
8.12	粵	紫釵記	雛鳳鳴粵劇團	霍小玉 李益	梅雪詩 龍劍笙	1984
8.13	粵	紫釵記	雛鳳鳴粵劇團	霍小玉	梅雪詩	1984
8.14	粵	紫釵記	雛鳳鳴粵劇團	黃衫客 霍小玉 浣紗	朱秀英 梅雪詩 任冰兒	1984
8.15	川	皮金滾燈	成都市芙蓉花川劇團	皮妻 皮金	蕭代芬 蘇明德	1988
8.16	川	皮金滾燈	成都市芙蓉花川劇團	皮金	蘇明德	1988
8.17	越	西廂記	浙江小百花越劇團	崔鶯鶯 張君瑞	陶慧敏 茅威濤	1991
8.18	越	西廂記	浙江小百花越劇團	張君瑞	茅威濤	1991
8.19	越	西廂記	浙江小百花越劇團	崔鶯鶯	陶慧敏	1991
8.20	越	西廂記	浙江小百花越劇團	崔鶯鶯 張君瑞	陶慧敏 茅威濤	1991
9.1	秦腔	殺狗勸妻	陝西青年秦腔劇團	焦氏 曹莊	蕭英 李小烽	1990
9.2	評	拾玉鐲	河北石家莊青年評劇團	孫玉姣	劉鳳芝	1991
9.3	粵	拾玉鐲	屯門實驗粵劇團	孫玉姣	陳秀卿	1981
9.4	評	拾玉鐲	河北石家莊青年評劇團	孫玉姣 劉媒婆	劉鳳芝 靳玲展	1991
9.5	評	劉伶醉酒	河北石家莊青年評劇團	劉伶	趙立華	1991
9.6	評	劉伶醉酒	河北石家莊青年評劇團	劉伶 杜康	趙立華 楊春利	1991
9.7	評	劉伶醉酒	河北石家莊青年評劇團	劉伶 杜康	趙立華 楊春利	1991
9.8	潮	王茂生進酒	廣東潮劇團	門官	柯立正	1984
9.9	潮	王茂生進酒	廣東潮劇團	門官 王茂生	柯立正 陳秦夢	1984
9.10	潮	王茂生進酒	廣東潮劇團	王茂生 薛仁貴 門官	陳秦夢 陳光耀 柯立正	1984
9.11	贛	竇娥冤	江西省贛劇團	竇娥 蔡婆	涂玲慧 熊麗雲	1992
9.12	贛	竇娥冤	江西省贛劇團	竇娥	涂玲慧	1992
9.13	贛	竇娥冤	江西省贛劇團	竇娥 竇天章	涂玲慧 李維德	1992
9.14	贛	夜夢冠帶	江西省贛劇團	崔氏	涂玲慧	1992
9.15	贛	夜夢冠帶	江西省贛劇團	崔氏	涂玲慧	1992

照片	劇　種	劇　目	劇　團	劇中人	扮演人	年份
9.16	贛	夜夢冠帶	江西省贛劇團	崔氏	涂玲慧	1992
9.17	晉	教子	山西省晉劇團	薛保 薛英哥 王春娥	趙小雷 李雲麗 栗桂蓮	1986
9.18	晉	教子	山西省晉劇團	薛英哥 王春娥	李雲麗 栗桂蓮	1986
10.1	川	白蛇傳	成都市川劇院三團	法海	孫普協	1991
10.2	京	醉打山門	遼寧青少年京劇團	賣酒人 魯智深	李小亮 趙輝	1986
10.3	京	醉打山門	遼寧青少年京劇團	魯智深 賣酒人	趙輝 李小亮	1986
10.4	京	醉打山門	遼寧青少年京劇團	魯智深 賣酒人	趙輝 李小亮	1986
10.5	徽	雙下山	安徽省徽劇團	悟明	張敏	1991
10.6	徽	雙下山	安徽省徽劇團	本無 悟明	許友升 張敏	1991
10.7	越	雙下山	寧紹小白花越劇團	悟明 本無	周淑君 潘琴	1990
10.8	越	游庵認母	上海越劇院紅樓劇團	志貞	金采風	1991
10.9	越	游庵認母	上海越劇院紅樓劇團	志貞 徐元宰	金采風 錢惠麗	1991
11.1	河北梆子	武松血濺鴛鴦樓	河北梆子戲劇團	武松	裴艷玲	1992
11.2	河北梆子	夜奔	河北梆子戲劇團	林沖	裴艷玲	1992
11.3	京	李逵探母	上海京劇院	李逵	尚長榮	1992
11.4	京	李逵探母	潘陽京劇院	李母 李逵	徐俊 汪慶元	1992
11.5	河北梆子	武松血濺鴛鴦樓	河北梆子戲劇團	武松	裴艷玲	1992
11.6	河北梆子	武松血濺鴛鴦樓	河北梆子戲劇團	武松	裴艷玲	1991
11.7	河北梆子	武松血濺鴛鴦樓	河北梆子戲劇團	蔣門神 武松	孫分田 裴艷玲	1991
11.8	河北梆子	武松血濺鴛鴦樓	河北梆子戲劇團	武松	裴艷玲	1992
11.9	河北梆子	武松血濺鴛鴦樓	河北梆子戲劇團	武松	裴艷玲	1992
12.1	秦腔	西湖遺恨	陝西青年秦腔劇團	李慧娘	李梅	1990
12.2	河北梆子	鍾馗嫁妹	河北梆子戲劇團	鍾馗 楊國松	裴艷玲 張峰山	1991
12.3	河北梆子	鍾馗嫁妹	河北梆子戲劇團	鍾馗	裴艷玲	1991
12.4	河北梆子	鍾馗嫁妹	河北梆子戲劇團	鍾馗	裴艷玲	1991
12.5	河北梆子	鍾馗嫁妹	河北梆子戲劇團	鍾馗	裴艷玲	1991

照片	劇　種	劇　目	劇　　團	劇中人	扮演人	年份
12.6	河北梆子	鍾馗嫁妹	河北梆子戲劇團	鍾馗 鍾梅英	裴艷玲 彭蕙蘅	1991
12.7	川	活捉三郎	成都市川劇院三團	閻惜姣 張三郎	田惠文 李增林	1991
12.8	川	活捉三郎	成都市川劇院三團	張三郎	李增林	1991
12.9	川	活捉三郎	成都市川劇院三團	閻惜姣 張三郎	田惠文 李增林	1991
12.10	粵	再世紅梅記	珠海粵劇團	裴禹	姚志強	1993
12.11	粵	再世紅梅記	珠海粵劇團	盧昭容 賈似道	白雪紅 關耀棠	1993
12.12	秦腔	西湖遺恨	陝西青年秦腔劇團	李慧娘 裴禹	蕭英 李小鋒	1990
12.13	秦腔	西湖遺恨	陝西青年秦腔劇團	李慧娘	蕭英	1990
12.14	川	狐仙恨	成都市川劇院三團	石懷玉	孫湧波	1991
12.15	川	狐仙恨	成都市川劇院三團	狐仙 石懷玉	陳巧茹 孫湧波	1991
12.16	川	狐仙恨	成都市川劇院三團	石懷玉 狐仙	孫湧波 陳巧茹	1991
12.17	粵	牡丹亭驚夢	雛鳳鳴粵劇團	春香 杜麗娘	任冰兒 梅雪詩	1984
12.18	粵	牡丹亭驚夢	雛鳳鳴粵劇團	柳夢梅 **杜麗娘**	龍劍笙 **梅雪詩**	1984
12.19	粵	牡丹亭驚夢	雛鳳鳴粵劇團	柳夢梅	龍劍笙	1984
12.20	潮	柴房會	廣東潮劇團	莫二娘 李老三	吳玲兒 方展榮	1991
12.21	潮	柴房會	廣東潮劇團	李老三	方展榮	1991
13.1	京	小上墳	遼寧青少年京劇團	劉景祿 蕭素貞	李小亮 管波	1986

Note: In this table, only the main performers or characters in the photographs are identified, from left to right or from top to bottom.

Select Bibliography

English-language Books

Buck, Pearl S., trans. *All Men Are Brothers.* Rev. ed. Taipei: Hsin Lou Publishing 1937

Crump, J.I. *Chinese Theatre in the Days of Kublai Khan.* Tucson: University of Arizona Press 1980

Dolby, William. *A History of Chinese Drama.* New York: Harper and Row 1976

—. *Eight Chinese Plays.* New York: Columbia University Press 1978

Fu Qifeng. *Chinese Acrobatics through the Ages.* Beijing: Foreign Languages Press 1985

Gao Ming. *The Lute.* Translated by Jean Mulligan. New York: Columbia University Press 1980

Hsu Tao-Ching. *The Chinese Conception of the Theatre.* Seattle: University of Washington Press 1985

Hung, Josephine Huang. *Classical Chinese Plays.* Taipei: Mei Ya Publications 1972

Lo Kuan-chung. *Romance of the Three Kingdoms.* Translated by C.H. Brewitt-Taylor. Chinese Classics Series in English. Taipei: Caves Publishing 1925

Mackerras, Colin. *Chinese Drama: A Historical Approach.* Beijing: New World Press 1990

—. *Chinese Theater.* Honolulu: University of Hawaii Press 1983

—. *The Chinese Theatre in Modern Times.* London: Thames and Hudson 1975

Tsao Hsueh Chin. *Dream of the Red Chamber.* Translated by Chi-Chen Wang. New York: Twayne Publishers 1958

Tung, Constantine, and Colin Mackerras. *Drama in the People's Republic of China.* Albany: State University of New York Press 1987

Wang Kefan. *The History of Chinese Dance.* Beijing: Foreign Languages Press 1985

Wu Ch'eng-en. *Monkey.* Translated by Arthur Waley. © John Day Company. New York: Grove Press 1943

Chinese-language Books

中國大百科全書總編輯委員會（1983）：中國大百科全書：戲曲曲藝 中國大百科全書出版社 北京

李漢飛 編（1987）：中國戲曲劇種手冊 中國戲曲出版社 北京

湯草元 陶雄 主編（1981）：中國戲曲曲藝詞典 上海辭書出版社 上海

周貽白（1978）：中國戲劇史 僶勉出版社　　台南

郭雲龍 校訂（1978）：中國歷代戲曲選 宏業書局有限公司 台北

曾白融 主編（1989）：京劇劇目辭典 中國戲曲出版社 北京

謝中編（1990）：越劇戲考 浙江人民出版社　　杭州

馬少波 章力揮 等（1990）：中國京劇史（上下卷）中國戲劇出版社 北京

Videotapes and Audiotapes

Video shops in overseas Chinese communities often stock Peking and Cantonese operas. These videos can be an excellent starting place for a sense of the sound and movement that accompany the photographs in this book. The following organizations are also good sources to follow up a particular opera style.

The Broadcasting Development Fund offers a number of regional operas and storytelling programs on video. 13th floor, #15-1, Section 1, Hang Chow South Road, Taipei, Taiwan 100, R.O.C.

Queen Records offers a variety of regional operas and storytelling programs on audio cassette. 4th floor, #9, 27 Lane, Shui Yuan Street, Yung Ho, Taipei County, Taiwan R.O.C.

Index

Falsetto singing, 18, 24, 33
Female characters (dan) 旦
    clowns, 37
    daomadan ('weapon and horse woman') 刀馬旦 33
    guimendan ('private-quarters woman') 閨門旦 33
    huadan (lively maiden) 花旦 33
    laodan (old woman) 老旦 33
    qingyi (young maiden) 青衣 33
    as type in Chinese opera, 5
    wudan (warrior woman) 武旦 33, 96
    See also Female impersonators; Women
Female impersonators, 9
Fiddle, 17, 18, 19, 22-3, 30
Fighting, in Chinese opera. See Martial arts, in Chinese opera
Finding Mother in a Convent 游庵認母 176-7
First fiddle (jinghu) 京胡 30
Flags, meaning of, 28
Floods, 28
Flute, 17, 18, 22, 23, 24, 31
Flying Tiger 孫飛虎 146
Folk music, 14
Fools, 5. See also Clowns
Fox fairies, 19, 202-3
Fu Peng 傅朋 152
Fujing 副淨 5
Fumo 副末 5

Gan (Jiangxi) opera. See Jiangxi (Gan) opera
Gang of Four, 10
Gao Junbao 高君保 102-3
Gao Ming 高明 8
Gaoqiang music 高腔 13
Generals
    operas about, 82-111
    and significance of flags, 28
    Yang generals, 18, 99
    See under full names
Gesture, in Chinese opera, 28
Ghosts
    in Chaozhou opera, 25
    operas about, 188-209
    in Sichuan opera, 19
Gift of Wine, A 王茂生進酒 158-60
Goddess of Mercy (Guanyin) 觀音 39, 57
Goddess of the Hundred Flowers 百花聖母 40
Goldfish Fairy 金魚仙子 50-1, 53
Great Wall of China, 65, 74
Great Warrior Dance, The (Dawu) 大武 4
Guan Hanqing 關漢卿 7, 161

Guan Xing 關興 94
Guan Yu 關羽 36, 83, 85, 87-8, 94-5
Guangdong province, 17, 24, 25
Guangguang opera. See Qin opera
Guanyin. See Goddess of Mercy
Guimendan ('private-quarters woman') 閨門旦 33
Guitar. See Moon guitar

Hai Jun 海俊 105-6
Haiyan music 海鹽 25
Han Chinese, 7-8, 79, 80, 105
Han dynasty 漢 83
Han Qi 韓琪 125-6
Hand clappers (ban) 板 19-20, 32
Harlequin, 6
Haunting of Zhang Sanlang, The 活捉三郎 195-7
Heaven
    in Chinese culture, 39
    and role of emperor, 65
Heavenly beings, operas about, 39-64
Heaven's Gate, 99
Hebei Clapper opera 河北梆子戲
    Burning the Camps 火燒連營 94-5
    Death at Prayer 吳漢殺妻 107-8
    Monkey Business in Heaven 鬧天宮 57
    Night Flight 夜奔 180
    Prince Lanling 蘭陵王 108-11
    stylistic elements, 15
    Wu Song's Revenge 武松血濺鴛鴦樓 183-7
    Zhong Kui Arranges a Marriage 鍾馗嫁妹 190-4
Hebei province, 15
Heilongjiang province, 14
Hibiscus Fairy 芙蓉花仙 40-3
Hibiscus Fairy, The 芙蓉花仙 40-3
'High melodic' troupes, 21
'High music,' 13
Hong Sheng 洪昇 9
Hongniang 紅娘 146
Hongsheng (red face) 紅生 36
Horn butting, 6
Hua Mulan 花木蘭 72
Huadan (lively maiden) 花旦 33
Huang of the Eastern Sea 東海黃公 6
Huangmei opera 黃梅戲
    Dream of the Red Chamber 紅樓夢 135-8
    stylistic elements, 22-3
Huangpu Shaohua 皇甫少華 72
Huarong Pass, The 華容道 87-8
Hui (Anhui) opera. See Anhui (Hui) opera
Hunan province, 17

Set in Trump Mediæval
Printed and bound in Hong Kong by Kings Time Industries Ltd.
Copy-editor: Camilla Jenkins
Designer: George Vaitkunas
Indexer: Annette Lorek
Proofreader: Robyn Packard